POETIC VOYAGES
EAST YORKSHIRE

Edited by Simon Harwin

First published in Great Britain in 2001 by
YOUNG WRITERS
Remus House,
Coltsfoot Drive,
Peterborough, PE2 9JX
Telephone (01733) 890066

HB ISBN 0 75433 100 8
SB ISBN 0 75433 101 6

FOREWORD

Young Writers was established in 1991 with the aim to promote creative writing in children, to make reading and writing poetry fun.

This year once again, proved to be a tremendous success with over 88,000 entries received nationwide.

The Poetic Voyages competition has shown us the high standard of work and effort that children are capable of today. It is a reflection of the teaching skills in schools, the enthusiasm and creativity they have injected into their pupils shines clearly within this anthology.

The task of selecting poems was therefore a difficult one but nevertheless, an enjoyable experience. We hope you are as pleased with the final selection in *Poetic Voyages East Yorkshire* as we are.

CONTENTS

East Halton Primary School

Rebecca Lawtey	73
Kellie North	74
Rebecca Tuner	75
Hazel Newton	75
Denise Parker	76
Adam Rowbotham	76
Holly Evans	77
Emma Turner	77

Hornsea CP School

Rachael Schofield	78
Kirsthy McNaughton	78
Louise Pannhausen	79
James Varley	79
Jessica Cox	80
Bryony Cox	80
Natalie Wardill	81
Samantha Chew	81
Darryl Eastwood	82
Adam Whitaker	82
Charlotte Empsall	83
Luke Naylor	83
Shaun Brooke	84
Michael Smith	84
Ben Asquith	85
Alannah Colley	85
Ashley Evans	86
Kerry Railton	86
Katie Russell	87
Anna-May Rogers	87
Louis Lawson	88
Ben Wallis	88
Kate Southey	89
Katie Robinson	89
Chris Hawksworth	90
Jayne Girling	90
Michael Prescott	91

Natalie Wilson	91
Ben Cheer	92
Ashleigh Bray	92
Shaun Taylor	93
Kayleigh Hampson	93
Alec Tomlinson	94
Daniel Roberts	94
Frances M Hackett	95
Michael Bradley	95
Thomas Read	96
Catherine Suret	96
Aaron Scott	97
Hollie Parnham Stevens	98
Chris Nicholson	98
Tom Prout	99
Michaela Armstrong	100
Amanda Ashburner	101
Sarah-Louise Gardener	102
Edward Naylor	103
Kelsie Wason	104
Kirsty Peck	105
Phil Taylor	106

Kingsway Primary School

Peter Jones	107
Dale Malcolmson	107
Sian Hastings	108
Natalie Wreakes	108

North Frodingham Primary School

April Boyes	109
David Edwards	109
Anne-Marie Edwards	110
Hollie Warren	110
Jane Howey	111
Matthew Rymaruk	111
Corey Wylie	112
Joseph Copeland	112

Claire Edwards	113
Korina Cullen	113
Hannah Harewood	114
James Pearson	114
Daniel Charlton	115
Jenny Howey	115
Courtney Lamb	115
Thomas Pearson	116
Laura Wilson	116
James Doyle	116
Adam Lamb	117
Lucy Garton	117
Russell Wylie	117
Rachel Spence	118
Kelly Salvage	118
Hannah Walker	119
Sarah Walker	119
William Doyle	120
John Wilkinson	120
Lucy Davies	121
Lucy Pickard	122

Laceby Stanford School

Christian Louis	123
Lauren Grice	123
Robyn Cordall	124
Daniel Wilson	124
Jessica Sleeth	125
Jessica Saville	126
Sarah Pearson	126
Ben Cook	127
Martin Bowes	127
Ben Leeming	128
Lauren Walker	128
Joshua Campbell	129
Chelsea Wheeler	130
Christopher Pinney	130
Christian Cherry	131

The Poems

TEACHERS

There are some strange teachers
They live at Minster school
There always talking and never walking
I'll tell you about a few.

Mrs Hardwick she's a Y5 teacher
Some say's she's a witch
But all in vain I think she's great
That poor old teacher from Minster.

Mr O'Donoghue he's the best
He's the funniest of the rest
He's really cool and not a fool
That poor old teacher from Minster.

Mr Fuller he can't sing
Although apparently
He's good on computers
If you're not smart he'll throw a dart
That poor old teacher from Minster.

Mrs Smith she is so great
She really likes her music
She sings and sings without any wings
That poor old teacher from Minster.

Mr Bray he is quite strict
And loves his eye contact
He loves his science and his reading
That poor old teacher from Minster.

Mrs Sadofsky she is nice
But if you really thought twice
She's got two sides and really not kind
That poor old teacher from Minster.

Kirstie Lyon (10)
Beverley Minster CE Primary School

WHITE SCAR CAVES

Under the ground,
Where the dead people live,
Witches heard waking from the dead.
Dribble running down the face of dread.
Her fingers poised ready for her chance . . .

Thunderous waterfall echoed loudly,
Hissing venomously and crashing into rocks.
River dodging the jagged rocks,
Snapping swiftly under frozen feet.

The devil lurking in the Battlefield Cavern,
ready to trickle saliva onto your heads.
Unlucky victims are turned to stone,
by the dreaded devil of the dead.

Petrified animals and terrified souls,
Screaming sounds of their moaning and groaning
                    at the people that pass by.
Tortured souls that wonder around at night,
Beware it's not a very nice sight!

Laura Gray (10)
Beverley Minster CE Primary School

SUMMER IS

Summer is where . . .
I play outside in the scorching sun
I eat freezing strawberry and orange icepops,
the juice drips down my arm.
Sizzling sausages and smoky bacon
Smell gorgeous smouldering on the barbecue.
I love summer best of all.

Steven Coates (10)
Beverley Minster CE Primary School

INSIDE A CAVE

Inside the cave,
Blackness drip, drip, drop.
Fast, flowing and furious waterfalls,
Cold, rushing water that roars.
Whispering wind blows and bounces
            against the lemon flowstone.
Echoes through the caverns.
Fingers, heads and teeth tearing away the walls,
Saliva dribbling from open mouths
                silently screaming.
The battlefield demolished by deadly bombs.
The Devil spitting,
His tongue thrusting through the ground,
A judge rising from the flowstone.
The waterfall like a dwarf's beard,
Flowing like hard froth.
Yet darkness is still.

Alex Revell (11)
Beverley Minster CE Primary School

THE SCHOOL PLAY

The school play is about Doris Day
It's called Calamity Jane.
The main character is a boy called Jay
So he's like a pantomime dame!

The school play is at the end of May
You don't even have to pay
So come along and join the fun
If you don't you will be feeling our gun!

Laura Coates (10)
Beverley Minster CE Primary School

MOUNTAIN BIKE

A jaw cracker
A mud splatterer
A brain buster
An arm cluster.

A back breaker
A body shaker
A bone chiller
A nerve driller.

A knee smasher
A rock masher
A leg basher
A chest dasher

Boy over handlebars!

Shashank Srirama (11)
Beverley Minster CE Primary School

MOUNTAIN BIKING

A butt basher
A mud masher
Knee knockers
Stone knock-us
A brake squeaker
Oil leaker
Chain cruncher
Tyre puncher
A skid spinner
A wheel winner
A metal machine
Fit to ride.

Jordan Clark (11)
Beverley Minster CE Primary School

THE STORMY BLACK-EYED HORSE

Why do you run through the fields shying up, stopping on
                                        hills,
You are a spirit, a shiny light.
But at the same time a stormy night.
You stamp your hooves till your shoes come loose.
Then off you go jumping logs enjoying your life.
Prancing and dancing you're very fine,
So please run round one more time.
Your big black eyes looking at me, thinking why am I
                                        not free?
Your mane's a ribbon, your back black silk,
Your star on your head is as white as milk.
Then you run at the speed of a car.
And sometimes I wish I was near not far,
From your blackcoated wilderness.
When I hear your hooves clatter
It sounds like something's really the matter.
Suddenly you shy up high.
And start to dance through the sky.
You look so beautiful and so kind.
There's one other thing you have, and that's a stubborn mind.
Oh please don't go you'll make me cry,
But then again you're wild not mine.

Emily Staveley (10)
Beverley Minster CE Primary School

THE SPECIAL STARS

The Special Stars always shine at night.
The Special Stars sparkle bright!
The Shooting Star is ready to crash
With a thump and a smash!

Jordan Wilkinson (9)
Beverley Minster CE Primary School

I HAD A DREAM

I had a dream about one scene
I had a dream about a lightning beam
I had a dream about a comet crashing from the sky
I had a dream about some twinkle in my eye
I had a dream about one long nail
I had a dream about a sea full of ale
I had a dream about a cheetah it was so fast
I had a dream about a fat elephant come last
I had a dream about a man in the midst of night
I had a dream about a man without sight.
I had a dream about a man with fire
I had a dream about a man that got higher.

Luke Monaghan (9)
Beverley Minster CE Primary School

MOUNTAIN BIKING

A belly shaker
A back breaker

A jaw jiggler
A head wriggler

A bum basher
A wheel smasher

A cheek wobbler
A body joggler

A leg bumper
A stone jumper.

Man overboard!

Esther Seaman (10)
Beverley Minster CE Primary School

CAVES

Down, down deep
Under the ground,
A soul moans like a tortured dragon,
The water rips aside the people of stone,
That the devil's tongue has dripped on.
The witches' fingers reaching out to its prey
                    (of human flesh)
Evil Dracula creeps out at night to play with the
hobgoblins that lurk around the stagmites,
The witches face breaks through and gleams like
                    cats eyes in the dark.
The river under rails chewing and oozing round your
                    feet
the bubbles curving round the spiny corners of the
Dark,
Black,
Underground!

Alice Ramsay (11)
Beverley Minster CE Primary School

MY NEW DOGGY

All dogs need house training,
but not as much as mine.
He barks all night until 6 o'clock
        in the morning,
but until 2 o'clock he will just start
                    snoring.
My new doggy just loves to play,
so I told him to go away!

Jessica Harmer (10)
Beverley Minster CE Primary School

MOUNTAIN BIKE

Bum buster
Mud cluster

Leg knotter
Wheel clatter

Body bashing
Helmet cracking

Shoe slosher
Knee knocker

Head banger
Bone breaker

Gear grinder
Ground finder

Trouser shredder
A nerve thriller.

Matthew Lochead (10)
Beverley Minster CE Primary School

SPIDER!

Spider, spider,
Right behind her.
Turn around.
She saw it on the ground.
She gave a scream,
and drowned it in some cream.
Poor little,
spider, spider.

Andrew Hickling (9)
Beverley Minster CE Primary School

WAR

War is very bloody
War is very horrible and bad
In war people die
If we have wars the earth will not be a nice place to live
In war people get diseases which can kill
In war it's muddy and wet
In war the people who are innocent get killed
In war the earth gets destroyed
In war towns and cities get blown up
We should not be fighting
We should make up and decide to have no more wars
We are mad to fight

War is Bad

Nicholas Richards (10)
Beverley Minster CE Primary School

MUD

Mud it's slushy it's mushy
Nice between your toes,
It runs through your fingers.

Mud glorious mud.
Hot worms and earwigs.
While I'm in the mood.
Cold bugs and crickets.
Mouldy cabbage and carrots.
What next is the question
Rich dogs have it boys
Indigestion!

Calum McElwee (10)
Beverley Minster CE Primary School

CREATURES OF THE NIGHT

My poem is about creatures of the night
and you can only see them with good eyesight.
Some of them have the gift of flight,
flying in the bright moonlight.

The badgers come right out of their set,
to find the grass all damp and wet.
They're not good to keep as a pet,
or to catch in a net.

. . . In the end the darkness goes away
and lets the sun come out to play.

Jenny Carmichael (10)
Beverley Minster CE Primary School

SMELLY SOCKS

Socks, socks,
Everywhere.

Smelly socks,
I don't care.

Socks!

Smelly socks,
very smelly.

Socks, socks,
Not as smelly as Jimmy's welly.

Smelly socks,
Normal socks.
Striped
    Socks!

Tom Parkin (9)
Beverley Minster CE Primary School

MOUNTAIN BIKE

A hair waver,
A fringe freezer.

A nose sniffler,
An eye stinger.

A teeth rattler
A mouth masher.

An arm jiggler
A shoulder clanger.

A bottom basher
A wheel bumper.

A leg wobblier,
A knee knocker.

Gruesome machine, just waiting to tip me
Up!

Francesca Hyde (11)
Beverley Minster CE Primary School

SUMMER IS ...

One of the best seasons,
It has the longest holiday.
The bees are buzzing in the sun,
Pretty flowers like to hide in the long grass.
The sun shines on the corn growing in the fields,
While the birds sing.
The strawberries grow where the beetles and worms
Crawl under the earth.
Rainbow ice cream melts in the sun.

Martin Overrill (10)
Beverley Minster CE Primary School

I SAW A DREAM

I saw a dream with a stallion as tall as the moon
I saw a removal at our new house we were leaving soon
I saw a comet drop out of the sky hot and blazing with fire.
I saw a shifty man so I knew the consequences would be dire.
I saw a very bright twinkly and glittery star.
I saw a man who owned a drinking bar.
I saw a woman who looked just like my double jump off a cliff
I saw a young couple having a lovers tiff.
I saw a beach sprinkled softly with sand which looks like silk.
I saw a baby drinking a bottle of milk.
I saw a fiddler playing a delicately soft tune
I saw a young man eating his lunch because it was noon.

Jessica Rossi (9)
Beverley Minster CE Primary School

MY TWIN BROTHERS

My twin brothers are little pests.
As they stood there wearing identical vests.
Somedays they are very good and somedays very bad,
They make my rip my hair out with frustration.
They make me very sad.
When my friends come round I do get embarrassed,
Because of their table manners.
And when my dad isn't looking, they're in the
garage stealing his useful spanners!
They're shouting at each other,
Breaking each other's stuff.
Oh I do love my twin brothers,
But sometimes I've had
     Enough.

Rachael Langley (10)
Beverley Minster CE Primary School

MY PET

Eyes like dew
on morning grass
oh so shiny like,
glistening diamonds.

Claws like tiny
glittering daggers,
so sharp they
could win a
battle any day.

With a shiny
black coat, lets
get the sunglasses.

Have you guessed
it's my cat, yes my cute
little cat.
Felix

Alex Rossi (9)
Beverley Minster CE Primary School

TIME

Time time 365 days in a year,
Time time twelve months in a year,
Time time four weeks in a month,
Time time seven days in a week,
Time time twenty four hours in a day,
Time time sixty minutes in an hour,
Time time sixty seconds in a minute,
Time time one hundred milliseconds in a second.
Time!

Iris Hardege (9)
Beverley Minster CE Primary School

THE WATERFALL

Up high in the valley her first splash is born,
From the same spring bursts cold, fresh water,
Gushing down after the first trickle,
Starting a stream of her own,
Although imprisoned in her banks,
Centuries later she breaks free,
She roars with excitement and rushes out,
Sweeping away anything in her path,
Finally she reaches the cliff,
Without looking back she throws herself down,
Bubbling with laughter, she has no fear,
As soon as she hits rock she explodes into a
                          fountain of spray,
Happy to be free she glides out to sea,
If you listen she's still laughing today . . .

Ruth Thompson (11)
Beverley Minster CE Primary School

CAVES

Thrusting through the rock
The devil rudely pokes his tongue
Wiggling from side to side
Water rushing to the ground
Splashing, Splashing as it drops
Dribbling saliva slashing at our cheeks
His fingers scratching at the wall
Stabbing with his nails
Warty fingers popping
Puss is squirming out
His calcite horn
Blood is dripping down.

Marc Wilson (11)
Beverley Minster CE Primary School

THUNDERSTORM

Traumatising thunderstorm,
Why do you haunt me?
Traumatising thunderstorm,
Why do you daunt me?

Terrifying thunderstorm,
Why do you chill me?
Terrifying thunderstorm,
Why do you thrill me?

Electric lightning,
Why do you scare me?
Electric lightning,
Why do you dare me?

Brilliant lightning,
Why do you fright me?
Brilliant lightning,
Why do you excite me?

Emma Dennison (9)
Beverley Minster CE Primary School

AUTUMN DAYS

The autumn leaves flicker in the gentle wind.
The misty sun hangs low in the morning sky.
The first sights of frost are on the pond.
The leaves change to the colours of the rainbow.
Brown, red, orange and gold.
The old cold nights when the wind whistles spookily through
the trees.
Summer has gone. Now it is the autumn days.

Joe Burke (10)
Beverley Minster CE Primary School

LOVE

Love is the colour of fairy pink and baby blue in a heart shaped
cloud.

Love smells like elegant flowers blooming into rainbows as
vivid as a painting.

Love tastes like creamy crystal ice-creams swirling
round the mouth.

Love sounds like dreamy butterflies flittering through
the gentle breeze.

Love feels dazzling and cheerful in the bright warm strawberry
heart.

Love lives in your life; it gleams like a cherry pie.

Holly Pratt (10)
Beverley Minster CE Primary School

A DEEP BLUE SEA

A deep blue sea,
with greasy seaweed all around me.

A deep blue sea,
With silver, and gold mermaids flowing
about with thee,

A deep blue sea,
With great white sharks looking at juicy fish
for tea.

A deep blue sea,
With white horses pounding almost killing me.

Katie Clark (10)
Beverley Minster CE Primary School

MY BEST FRIEND DAISY

My Best Friend has claws
At the end of her paws.
She's a friend for all witches.
And her tail really twitches.

She has pointed ears,
And I laugh till there's tears.
As she tries to catch flies,
Cos I know she really tries.

My Best Friend has fur
And all she does is purr.
She's lovely and fluffy,
And she never gets huffy.

Can you guess who?
I bet you can to!
My Best Friend is my cat,
And she just sits on the mat.

Sophie Townsend (11)
Beverley Minster CE Primary School

MIDNIGHT

Midnight strikes at twelve o'clock.
Santa comes at midnight on Christmas Eve,
        and eats his mince pies.
The tooth fairy comes at midnight too.
Midnight has ended and it's morning now.
Midnight has come once more and it starts
        all over again.

Andrew Fraser (9)
Beverley Minster CE Primary School

THE DRAGON SLAYER

There was a man who slaughtered dragons,
In cold and dark and misty caverns,
One day he found the mighty Borg,
Whom he planned to slaughter with a sword.

His plan though clever - went badly wrong
For a while he whistled a merry song
The dragon hid in his lagoon,
The man knew nothing of his doom.

Without a sound, old Borg crept closer,
Then Borg burned him like a toaster,
'At last!' Borg said, 'I've killed the man,
And ruined his nasty treacherous plan.'

But then . . .

Another man who slaughtered dragons,
In cold and dark and misty caverns,
'I'll kill old Borg,' he bravely boasted,
Alas, our friend was also toasted.

Robin Clayton (10)
Beverley Minster CE Primary School

WHAT IS?

What is pink?
A tulip's pink when I wink.
What is blue?
The sky is blue whilst the cows go moo.
What is red?
Death is red whilst I am in the shed.

Sarah Partridge (10)
Beverley Minster CE Primay School

THE WATERFALL

Waterfall shook as shiny face
spat out foam
Irrigate to a different place.

It cuts through rocks and makes
them smooth
leaves behind debris
to bring along with it.

I shot a cold stare
Froze the river
till it was like ice.

In winter he walks to
his finest bed
he does not wake until Spring.

James Neville (11)
Beverley Minster CE Primary School

I WISH . . .

I wish I lived in a castle far far away,
I wish I had all the TY Beanies and didn't have to pay.
I wish I could be in Harry Potter,
And be a *Great* Philosopher.
And wish I could be on television and have lots of fame.
And everyone in the world knew my name.
I wish I could record my own single.
I'll see all the stars and start to mingle
I wish I had a talking dog!
That can guide me through when I'm walking through
fog.

Charlotte Boyce (10)
Beverley Minster Primary School

LATE

I'm late for my friend's party,
It's pouring down with rain.
My dad's at work, he's got the car,
My head has got a pain.

I'm running around in circles,
Where did I put my dress?
I cannot find my make-up,
My hair is one big mess.

My mum tells me to calm down,
I'm really going insane.
My hair is all so tatty,
It's like a lion's mane.

I'm bumping into shelves,
One has fallen down!
The party is far away,
The other end of town.

I've knocked Kelly over,
My stupid little sis.
She said I should be careful,
I think that one's a miss!

My tummy has just turned over,
I'm going in a spin.
Where is the box of cookies?
They aren't in the cookie tin!

Tommy's in my room now,
Where did I put my dress?
There is my best make-up,
Oh No! He's made a mess!

I'm late for my friend's party!

I think I'm going to faint.

Sarah White (9)
Beverley Minster CE Primary School

MRS SUMMERS THINKS I'M . . .

Mrs Summers thinks I'm listening
but I'm really being a mermaid,
with my best friend,
the sealife plays with us,
Seals, fish and even more mermaids;
We swim with dolphins.
There's a storm we meet handsome fish
We get married and have spry
We are one big family.

Mrs Summers thinks I'm working
But I'm Britney Spears
Bodyguards around me
I'm shopping in London
Going in all the designer shops,
Gap, Morgan, River Island and Disney Store.
I have dinner in Harrods and get toys from Hamleys.
Prince William invites me around.
I wake up.
Mrs Summers' standing beside me tapping her foot
                              on the ground.

Aimee Smedley (11)
Beverley Minster CE Primary School

WEREWOLF

On a dark spooky, night,
With a full moon in sight.
An ordinary girl,
Takes a twirl,
Then the transformation begins,
She fights it but the doggy side wins.
She swipes her claws and the window
breaks,
And runs like mad with the wind she takes.
The wolf hurt a lot of people,
Especially the vicar that owned the local steeple.
She runs through the gloomy woods,
The hunter has a gun with a silver bullet,
He finds the wolf and the trigger, he pulls it!
He could have given her an antidote,
But, just for money he cut her throat.

Sophie Flockton (10)
Beverley Minster CE Primary School

HAPPINESS

Happiness is the colour of a sun with a
blazing hot yellow.
Happiness has a colourful smell of fresh strawberries.
It tastes like juicy tropical fruits flowing down your throat.
Happiness sounds like joy and laughter.
Happiness feels like a scorching sun.
Happiness lives in your heart and dreams.

Laura Child (9)
Beverley Minster CE Primary School

DAYDREAMING

Mrs Summers thinks I'm working -
but no, I'm kickboxing in America
or playing in the NBA.

I'm falling down a cliff,
and I land in all the money on earth.

Mrs Summers thinks I'm reading
but no, I'm in a western killing all the baddies,
or gliding through the wind.

I'm climbing up a mountain,
I get to the top and win 10,000 pounds.

Mrs Summers thinks I'm listening
but no I'm on WF Smackdown,
or I'm a superhero with ultimate strength.

I'm flying through space in a rocket,
and I land on an alien inhabited planet.
I Wish!

Josh Meredith (10)
Beverley Minster CE Primary School

THE SUN

Sunbathe
next to the pool
feel the warmth of the sun
eat lots of ice cream and drink lots
So hot.

Tamsyn Larvin (11)
Beverley Minster CE Primary School

THE 'ANIMAGUS'

The 'Animagus' is a very powerful spell,
What exactly it does no one can tell.
All we know is that it does strange things
It might turn them into a creature with wings.

These people we speak of are very strong,
Although they have done nothing wrong.
Potter, Lupin, Pettigrew and Black,
Beware . . . they will attack!

A werewolf, a snake, a dog, a cat,
A pigeon, a fly, a mouse, a rat.
The whomping willow that holds their secret,
Be careful it can give you a knee cut.

I cannot tell you any more,
Because it will make you sore.
If you want to know the rest, you rotter,
I suggest you read *Harry Potter!*

Helen Thompson (10)
Beverley Minster CE Primary School

INSIDE MY HEAD

Mr Bray thinks I'm reading, but I'm racing trains in a
sports car.

Mr Bray thinks I'm writing, but I'm wrestling
crocodiles in a swamp.

Mr Bray thinks I'm drawing, but I'm jumping out of a
plane 6000 feet high, far, far away, from Mr Bray!

Tom Frankland (10)
Beverley Minster CE Primary School

MRS SUMMERS THINKS . . .

Mrs Summers thinks I'm working
but really I'm sky diving
or killing jumps with a crosser.
In my spare time I'm coming off jumps
I could be hitting jumps with a BMX.
I might be ordering the teachers around
Or using the paraglide or parachute
hitting the quad around the mansion.
If you want to find me I might be
smashing the ice at the North Pole or
striding through the cool snow at a
competition or gliding through air
bungee jumping off the Golden Gate Bridge.

James Holden (11)
Beverley Minster CE Primary School

ANGRY WATERFALL

Angry waterfall thundering down.
Gush, crash, bang
Pushing the rock until it gets lower.

He can't get down the
rocks too strong.
He wails help!
I am scared of heights.

Some waterfalls push
the life from the rock,
blood went everywhere,
the rock fell down
the cliff! Bang! Kaboom!

Philippa Tate (10)
Beverley Minster CE Primary School

LITTLE HAMSTER

Little hamster
Cream and white,
Feeds and plays
Through the night.

Then through the day
When I'm at school,
He sleeps soundly
As a rule.

When I get home,
I clean him out,
Give him food
And he plays about.

He runs round
Quickly on his wheel,
And never never
Makes a squeal.

He makes his bed
In a nest of straw.
Then curls up
In a little ball.

David Worthington (10)
Beverley Minster CE Primary School

EAST YORKSHIRE

Mrs Summers thinks I'm reading
I'm actually eating toffee in sweet land.
Or travelling back in time.
I am skateboarding in the championship
And then I run in the Olympics.
I come home with two medals.

Mrs Summers thinks I'm working,
But no,
I'm scoring goals for Leeds Utd.,
then being man of the match.
I'm winning the lottery
And buying an Aston Martin.

James Stott (10)
Beverley Minster CE Primary School

MAD WATERFALL

The river rushing round bends
Up in the hills,
He turns the corner
Collides with a rock
His teeth shoot out like foam.

The river gets bigger
Water gets more violent as he crashes
against feeble rocks
He tumbles down drops in the hillside.

Then he sees the drop
What he has been waiting for all his life
He goes down roaring
Smash! He hits the bottom and savagely
Zooms down the rapids.

He cuts his long arms
on the rocks,
as he goes downstream
bloodthirsty he cuts his way through the
                    jagged stones
Until another waterfall comes along
Then it will start all over again.

Joe Seddon (11)
Beverley Minster CE Primary School

PLUMP WATERFALL

Summer strikes waterfall- hide, hide,
trees, other waterfalls laugh at his plumpness.

Autumn blows over - waterfall splash, crash,
waterfall becomes happier and happier.

Winter shivers around - waterfall slide, slide,
be happy and ignore the spitting tease.

Spring is born - waterfall rush, gush,
waterfall learns to ignore.

Fun and bounce, laughter and joy are what matters.

Summer rises again - *No* hide, *No* tease,
slide, ride, rush and gush, to the warm and gentle
breeze.

Katie Morris (10)
Beverley Minster CE Primary School

WATERFALL'S POEM

Lonely, sad waterfall cries.
His tears viciously spurt down the bare rocks.
Frustrated, water powerfully crashes down.

Destroys the creatures all around.
Hopelessly moaning in the scary black night.
Nobody hears his desperate cries.

He becomes more violent and awakens
other calm waterfalls.
Eventually he dies away, softly crying for help.

Holly Witty (10)
Beverley Minster CE Primary School

F50

Faster than a speeding bullet it whizzes round the track,
It shoots round cops corner at Silverstone and onto the
                    starting rack.
It flies into the pitstop and the engineer comes through the door.
It whizzes - whizzes - whizzes
It whizzes round the track once more.

It comes to the pitstop for a change of tyres.
It goes up to the Diablo and asks for a race.
So here they are at the starting line and ready for the race.
Their engines are roaring angrily out loud.
There's a sudden screech and a cloud of smoke
The race began, but where is the Diablo, its engine stalled
                    somehow.

Oliver Parker (10)
Beverley Minster CE Primary School

VOLCANOS

Sizzle! went the fearsome flaming hot fire.
Crackle! The hot red spitting lava desire.
Hissing! The hazy bubbling smoke covering thy
                    cool air.
Booming! The volcano erupting, the fire exploding wildly.
Fizzle! The heat of a thousand flames.
Whoosh! The rocks rumble and tumble from the volcano.
Bang! The rocky earth is dying down, down, down.
Splash! lava spills over thy edge of the volcano.
Pouring! All over the ground - red, orange, black, covering
                    thy earth.

Yasmin Eagle (10)
Beverley Minster CE Primary School

DINOSAUR JACK

Dinosaur Jack was full of woe;
from his spiky hair to his very large toe,
He hadn't had lunch he hadn't had tea
And wandered about hungrily.

He looked for plants or leaves up high;
Or something more tasty that might run by,
What could he see? What could he find?
He looked in front as well as behind.

Suddenly now from behind some rocks
Came a fast moving creature out of its blocks,
It looked very tasty it looked very lean,
The best looking meal that Jack had seen.

Time for some action time for a thrill,
Closing in slowly then in for the kill,
But Jack is a softy a really nice guy
Jack wouldn't but couldn't hurt a fly.

He weighed fifteen tons and was twenty feet tall;
He made everyone around him look extremely small,
Jack was the leader, head of the pack,
Everyone followed him no turning back.

Must stay together all safe and sound;
Until we arrive at the nesting grounds.

Natalie Bennyworth (10)
Beverley Minster CE Primary School

THE NONSENSE MAN

He puts soap on his toothbrush and toothpaste on his face,
He ties up his coat and he zips up his lace.
He puts jam in his tea and milk on his toast,
He opens his body and dresses the post.

He bathes in the sink and cleans his teeth in the bath,
He walks up the wall and he paints the path.
He stands on the mirror and looks in the floor,
He opens his pencils and draws with the door.
He is the nonsense man that is for sure.

Amy Eade (10)
Beverley Minster CE Primary School

CATS!

House Cats

They creep they crawl they purr,
They're sweet and soft and they care,
They're cute and cuddly and they sleep
                    in a tyre.
And when they're happy they go purr-purr-purr.
And then go purr curled up near the fire.

Street Cats

They're scary and creepy they live on the street,
They're rough and tough and not nice to meet.
They're greedy and smelly, they will eat anything
And when they're unhappy they scratch-scratch-scratch.

Lion

They live in the jungle and they are fierce,
Through the buffalo's neck the lion's teeth will pierce.
The lion sound is very loud,
Through the jungle they roar-roar-roar
With a shiny mane they stand very proud.

Sophie Bryan (9)
Beverley Minster CE Primary School

BONFIRE NIGHT

Lightning thunders from the sky,
On the crowded eve of bonfire night,
Rockets, bangers and jumping jacks
Whoosh into the sky.
Screaming, shouting and brightly
coloured fireworks zooming into the
air
Sticky toffee apples candyfloss like
pink clouds being munched by little
children.
Guy Fawkes is engulfed by
crackling fire as the red hot flames
dance around him,
Apples crunched,
Sweets all gone,
And the fire dies down,
Until another year.
Silence.

Alice Jones (9)
Beverley Minster CE Primary School

BUBBLE GUM

I like bubble gum, bubble gum's the best.

I like bubble gum, especially the strawberry flavour.

I like bubble gum, because you can
flick it, lick it, and twist it.

I like bubble gum it's as sweet as a fizzy lemon.

I like bubble gum.

Kimberley Hunt (10)
Beverley Minster CE Primary School

PERRIN THE DOG

When I have fallen down and hurt my knee,
Perrin the dog came up to me.
He sits close by and licks my hand
He always seems to understand.

When daddy's scolded me and said
'I'm cross with you go up to bed'
Perrin the dog comes with me too
And that's a friendly thing to do.

When I am frightened in the night,
Because I haven't any light
Perrin the dog is sure to creep
Beside my bed till I am asleep.

Alexandra Ellis (9)
Beverley Minster CE Primary School

PIRATES!

The pirate ship at Dover,
Is quite a sight to see,
With its many cannons,
You'll want to run and flee.

As the pirates climb aboard,
They drop the creamy sail,
Many of them shout and yell,
To pass that hammer and nail!

When the Captain gives the order,
They lift the gangplank high;
When they start to leave the port
They navigate by the sky.

Rory Fairbairn (9)
Beverley Minster CE Primary School

THE UNICORN

Cantering on a golden green,
Shaking its silver mane.
Rolling around in the blazing sun,
And dancing in the rain.

The spring it comes and blossom does fall,
Its horn it starts to glow,
Everything that winter froze,
Is back and flowers grow.

A wicked king who lived nearby,
Heard of this magic horn,
The unicorn was sent to die,
And buried in the thorns.

And till this day in magic lands
The horse is said to roam.
Still said to linger in the sun,
Still searching for a home.

Bronwyn Ellis (9)
Beverley Minster CE Primary School

FEAR

Fear is a crystal white ghost, floating through the gloom,
Fear smells like wheezy smoke waiting to strangle your neck,
Fear tastes of slimy sizzling acid poured down your throat,
Fear sounds like spirits screaming your name,
Fear feels like spine-chilling winds flowing inside you.
Fear lurks in a dark, crackling fire urging the flames to burn you
                                                        up.

Rachael Sims (10)
Beverley Minster CE Primary School

F1

Faster than the speed of light
It won't give up with a fight
Faster . . . faster . . . faster.
Cuts around the corner once more.
Its wheels skidding on the floor.
Faster . . . faster . . . faster.

It speeds along with all its might
Oh my God what a sight.
Faster . . . faster .. . faster.
Here comes the puma
For the overs he's a dume.
Faster . . . faster . . . faster.

Faster than the speed of light
It won't give up without a fight.
Faster . . . faster . . . faster
Cuts round the corner once more.
Its wheels skidding on the floor.

David Murrell (9)
Beverley Minster CE Primary School

SWEETS SHOP

I go to the sweet shop
The sweets look very nice.
They sell liquorice allsorts,
Strawberry pencils and gummy woodlice.

I go to the butchers hoping for a sweet.
I went to the butchers and all they sold
was meat.

Harry Bignell (10)
Beverley Minster CE Primary School

THE WIND

The wind darts to and fro,
Through the trees it blows,
Dances round the trees,
And floats up to the sea,
And floats up-up-up,
Up to the big blue sky.

The wind flies down the path,
And pushes the old ugly raft.
The wind freezes ponds and rivers,
And flies and dithers,
And dies down-down-down,
Right into the ground.

The wind whistles in your ear,
That's all that you can hear,
The sun starts to come out,
The wind has a doubt,
The wind goes-goes-goes,
The wind goes.

Stephanie Donkin (10)
Beverley Minster CE Primary School

WATERFALL

If the waterfall was a person,
She would be a singing
        a song happy.
As she dances around
Playing her drum fast and bashing
                    powerfully.

Michelle Robinson (10)
Beverley Minster CE Primary School

MRS SUMMERS THINKS I'M LISTENING BUT I'M . . .

Beating James Bond at poker
Doing jumps on my red crosser
Diving off a water fall
Scoring the winning try Hull FC.

Playing with a white tiger cub
Sand surfing in the desert
Trashing the Empire State building
Beating Kane in a hardcore match
Doing a hundred and ten miles per hour down the wrong side of the
road.

Drinking fifty pints of beer
Arresting ten druggies
Blowing up ten buildings
Climbing Mount Everest
I was really working the whole time . . . She thinks.

James Hood (11)
Beverley Minster CE Primary School

HAPPINESS

Happiness is yellow as the sun rising on a bright
summer morning.
Happiness smells like patches of violets growing in a
purple field.
It is the smell of the wind in the clouds
Happiness is the taste of cold jelly flavours in the warm
summer sun.
It smells like freshly cut grass ground beneath your feet
It feels like a calming calypso when everyone's smiling.
Happiness lives in the land of the magical hearts.

Megan Coates (10)
Beverley Minster CE Primary School

CATS

Running along a very high wall,
Kicking along its favourite ball.
Bounce, bounce, bounce it goes,
Bounce, bounce, bounce.
Kicking it along with its toes.

A bird swoops down past the wall,
Where the cats play with the ball.
Swoop, swoop, swoop, it goes,
Swoop, swoop, swoop.
Like a river it flows.

The bird comes to try its luck,
But the cat is pouncing look!
Pounce, pounce, pounce, it goes,
Pounce, pounce, pounce.
Now it is licking its toes.

James Turner (10)
Beverley Minster CE Primary School

SCARY CRITTERS

Scary Critters looking for lunch
Scary Critters living in the Deep.
Scary Critters, Carnivores in the Heap.
Scary Critters making a web.
Scary Critters at the dead.
Scary Critters at my head
Scary Critters coloured and scary
Scary Critters vile and hairy
Scary Critters.

Ben Scott (10)
Beverley Minster CE Primary School

MRS SUMMERS THINKS I'M READING . . .

But I'm on top of the pops singing my songs . . .

I'm going forward in time looking at my
future songs and reading them to my class . . .

Mrs Summers thinks I'm listening . . .
But I'm under the waves sending the
fish to sleep with my lullabies . . .

I'm sending the world a message of
Never ending love with my verses . . .

The planet is my universe of songs . . .

Jonty Bradbury (10)
Beverley Minster CE Primary School

MY GUINEA PIG

I have a guinea pig
Her name is Spotty,
She likes to eat things like apples and carrots,
And a lot more.

Sometimes she gets very hyper,
Sometimes she doesn't move,
She has a little face,
And she has little feet.

She is very old,
She's not very young,
She's really good,
I'm just glad she's mine.

Tom Beckley (10)
Beverley Minster CE Primary School

ANIMALS

A dolphin all shiny blue,
The cows in the meadows go moo.

A dog likes to have fun
An elephant weighs a ton.

A fish is colourful and scaly
I used to know a dog called Kaley.

I saw a mouse grey and very tiny,
I saw a fish very colourful and scaly.

I saw a monkey swing across the trees,
Once a goat stole my keys.

Allana Ross (9)
Beverley Minster CE Primary School

THE PLUG

The group of trees swaying their
Branches to put the plug in the
                    Rocks.

Turn on the water, but that was
A Mistake, the water runs through
The rocks, harming all the creatures
                    Around.

It runs through the villages,
Through the cities, until
It comes to the sea, at the bottom
Of a waterfall it is caught by the
Sea hands, and then it is put
With the rest of the water.

Jenny Granger (10)
Beverley Minster CE Primary School

NIGHT FRIGHT!

The sun was setting in the sky.
In front of the rusty moon,
Ghosts in the old streets,
Wolves with bright red eyes,
Foxes are hunting for chickens,
Eagles looking for rabbits,
The boy was having nightmares
About the horrible things,
The little boy was scared, scared, scared,
The little boy was scared about the horrible things,
The owl was making squeaking noises,
In the dirty trees,
The little boy scared, scared, scared,
The little boy was scared, about the horrible things.

Adam Waller (9)
Beverley Minster CE Primary School

THE FIRE CAT

In a big warm house
Sleeping near the fire lay
A big fat black and white cat
Purring like mad.

On a big puffy cushion
On a cold shivery winter's night.
Cats fed every hour
Cats cuddled everyday and night.

That cat is lovely
never scratches or fights
on a dark cold winter's night.

Hannah Bumford (9)
Beverley Minster CE Primary School

MOULDY MONDAY

Mouldy Monday was the day,
With teacher not yet there!
So Rachael, Sophie, Jazz and me
Decided to have a fair.

First it was the talent show
Which was a big mistake
Sophie decided to sing
A song a risky thing to take,
In order that she could be seen
She climbed upon a chair
And being a natural clumsy girl
Her trousers she did tear.

Racheal started laughing

And leant upon the door,
The door then hit the computer desk
Knocking it to the floor.

Jazz started worrying she didn't
Know what to do
I then had a brainwave I knew just what to do

Stick a drawing on the screen
To make it look like new.

Helena Magee (10)
Beverley Minster CE Primary School

THE SHOOTING STARS

Shooting stars glide in dark night sky
As they're gleaming in your eye.
With their silvery gleaming trail
They look like a sparkly nail.

With their great looks
They make me read my star books
With their bumpy backs
They look like dinosaur tracks.

Joe Oldroyd (9)
Beverley Minster CE Primary School

2468

2468 Who do we appreciate?
In the crowd watching the game,
Every Saturday's always the same.

5678 Hurry up or we'll be late.
Walking towards the ground in a big crowd,
We turn the corner, it sounds very loud.

1357 The stadium looks like Heaven.
The match begins at 3 o'clock,
The players come out in a big flock.

1234 Hull City are about to score,
Corners free kicks penalties too,
All on the pitch in front of you.

0369 It's half time. The players go off in a
                              neat line.
A foul, a free kick, the players make a wall,
The free kick taker strikes the ball.

268,10 Hull City score again.
The whistle goes the crowd roar,
2 Nil to City a brilliant score.

1543 Let's go home for tea.

Michael Starkey (10)
Beverley Minster CE Primary School

MOLLY

Molly, my rabbit is a wally,
And I love it.
She hardly sleeps through the night,
'Cos she's always scratching, scratching
Scratching, but hardly does she bite.

We always let her out in the garden,
And sometimes she runs to my friend Luke Pardon.
She likes hiding in the bushes,
And all we can hear is rustling, rustling,
Rustling, but she never ever rushes

We bring her in the house.
And she likes to catch the odd mouse.
My sister has a friend called Bess.
And Molly loves biting, biting.
Biting, and Molly loves biting,
My sister's friend's dress.

Dan Douglass (9)
Beverley Minster CE Primary School

MY STAR

I saw a star one night,
This one was gleaming and shining.
The star I saw was floating across the moon.
This one was bright yellow like no other star.
I could not bear to stop looking at it.
This one was special to me,
It was going faster now!
Then at last it disappeared.

Chelsea Carrick (9)
Beverley Minster CE Primary School

FOOTBALL

The kick of a ball on football field
What a blocking shield.
What a run, has a shot, what a striking goal,
Kicking, block,
Kicking, block,
The goal was scored by a player called Andy Cole.

What a cracking save.
The keeper was ever so brave.
What a run from Beckham,
run, run, run, run.
What a run from Beckham.
Watching the defenders come.

Scholes has some shots
It's England verse the Scots.
The defender is Sol Campbell
England, England, England
The Scots team is a shamble.

Sean Hughes (10)
Beverley Minster CE Primary School

MY RABBIT

I have a Rabbit
He's cute and cuddly
His name is Thumper
He has so much fur
You would think he's fat
But he's Thumper my Rabbit.
And I love him so that's
            That.

Samantha Gay (10)
Beverley Minster CE Primary School

MY MUM AND DAD

My mum and dad they're completely boring,
My dad is only good at drawing.

My mum she's a servant, the best,
She never gets a second for rest.

My dad he's always on his mobile phone,
He never gets any time for home.

My mum she's regular, when I say that I mean boring,
My dad's an expert in loud snoring.

My Mum and Dad They're Completely Boring.

Emma Anderson (9)
Beverley Minster CE Primary School

THE LITTLE PLACE TO PLAY

There was a little place to play,
Where children and their parents stay.
They lie and sit till sun has gone,
and don't regret what they have done.

When sun has gone and night did fall,
you can hear the owls call and call.
When you look up at the night sky,
you can't see many birds go by.

Now suddenly the morning dawned,
When everyone got up and yawned.
They all went to the place to play,
Where children and their parents stay.

Jodie Wilson (9)
Beverley Minster CE Primary School

THE UNENDING STAIRS

The unending stairs stairs go up and up,
Twisting, turning never stops.
Till we go up in the cloud!
Past a plane roaring loud.

The unending stairs never stop,
Up in space, now that's a lot!
An astronaut on the moon,
Our parents said to be back soon.

We wave goodbye,
And say farewell,
To all we've seen.
What a great time it has been.

We turn around and troop back down,
past the moon, the plane and cloud.
To the bottom round the bend,
of the stairs that never end.

Stuart Blucke (10)
Beverley Minster CE Primary School

RABBIT ON THE RUN

Running through the bushes and trees on the
Way knocked her knees as she talks to
Some friends running around the hutch.

She talked to her best friend Squeak the Guinea pig
                    as eating some broccoli.
Munch munch munch
Squeak Squeak Squeak
My rabbit's name's Buttons.

Jessica Barnett (9)
Beverley Minster CE Primary School

THE PINK PIG

The little pink pig eats an apple,
They live quite near the chapel,
He has a funny sound oink, oink, oink.
He is very sweet
But the only thing is a lot they eat.

The pink pig goes on a journey every day,
                    snorting away.
Then he goes to the farm,
The children he doesn't harm,
He smiles for a while

Then he goes to sleep,
Without making a peep,
He wakes up the next day,
The children shout hooray!

Amber Bryant (10)
Beverley Minster CE Primary School

THE ROLY-POLY BIRD

The roly-poly bird,
Is a very weird creature,
By night he's an explorer,
And by day he's a water feature.

He is also a colourful creature,
That tries his very best,
Because he lays square eggs,
In order to keep them in the nest!
(And by the way he hops!)

Cathrine Parr (9)
Beverley Minster CE Primary School

An Impatient Waterfall

A horrendous gushing lightning strike,
A person is having a fight,
Blood is flying everywhere rapids like a fair.

A trickle of a tear is falling off the pier,
And landing in a frustrated beach.
The rock pools are calm until the nasty, gushing,
mysterious target comes along.

The hair of the target is flying fast but a bit too fast
                to stop and harm anyone.

Eventually the target gets tired and goes to bed,
Until the sun comes to head.

Claire Whitfield (11)
Beverley Minster CE Primary School

Creepy Crawlies

Creepy crawlies on the floor
Creepy crawlies through the door
Creepy crawlies up the stairs
Creepy crawlies stand in pairs
Creepy crawlies with lots of hairs
Creepy crawlies as small as flairs
Creepy crawlies tickle your hair
Creepy crawlies are everywhere.

Lewis Northen (10)
Beverley Minster CE Primary School

ANGER

Anger is red like the colour of a burning lava pool
Anger smells like your hot blood ready to explode
It tastes like a rotten egg in a dirty dustbin
It sounds like a car crusher making you thin
It feels like roaring thunder striking you apart
Anger lies in the deepest depths of your heart.

Nattaphorn Price (10)
Beverley Minster CE Primary School

HOPE

Hope is the colour of a sparkling yellow.
Hope smells like a fresh sense coming into the world.
Its taste is warm and gentle to smooth your throat.
The sound of hope is caring for one another.
What hope feels like is to *Never* give up.
Hope lives in a friendly place where no one can destroy.

Imogen Fryer (10)
Beverley Minster CE Primary School

A PRETTY YOUNG LADY

A pretty young lady called Splatt
Sat on a mat with her cat
He bit her fat head,
Until she was dead,
Now what do you make of that?

Rachael Brooman (10)
Beverley Minster CE Primary School

MY CUDDLY FRIEND

W ith his pink tongue he drinks water,
E ating juicy apples by the quarter,
B est of all I like his bob tail
S hiny and fast, never like a snail,
T eeth that are gleaming white,
E ars that lay down at night,
R *abbit!*

Jessica Horner (9)
Beverley Minster CE Primary School

THERE WAS A YOUNG LADY

There was a young lady called Mary
She thought she was a fairy
She flew away
Then came back one day
But other people thought she was scary.

Sam White (11)
Beverley Minster CE Primary School

EARTH

Magical, blue,
Spinning, gliding, revolving,
Beautiful place to go,
Universal.

Jamie Wharam
Boothferry Primary School

IDENTITY TAG

I know a man who's got an identity tag.

He found it and he carried it
          during the war.
He found it and he carried it
when he shot the German soldier.
He found it and he carried it
when the soldier died of his wounds.
And he carried it and he carried it
for days and days and days.

I know a man who's got an identity tag
and he keeps it in a cupboard.
It's small and dull - nothing much to look at
but I think of the things he thinks
when he sees it:
how he found it
how he carried it
how he had to kill to live for it.

A small dull identity tag
worn always in war
and he keeps it in his drawer
to look at now and then.

Nicola Payne, Katie Scaife & Andrew Skirrow
Boothferry Primary School

MOON

Grey, small,
Glowing, sparkling, travelling,
Magical in the night,
Universal.

Liam Braithwaite
Boothferry Primary School

MEDAL

I know a man who's got a full set of medals.

He risked his life for them as he fought for them
                during the war.
He risked his life for them as he fought for them
when soldiers were dying all around him.
He risked his life for them as he fought for them
when his world was being destroyed.
And he fought for them and he fought for them
                for days and days and days.

I know a man who's got a full set of medals
and he keeps them in his drawer.
They're tarnished and dull - nothing much to look at
but I think of the things he thinks
when he sees them:
how he risked his life for them
how he fought for them
how his world was destroyed.

Tarnished dull medals
given for lives that were taken
and he keeps them in his drawer
to look at now and then.

Daniel Topliss & Oliver Turner
Boothferry Primary School

MOON

Silver, ghostly,
Sparkling, spinning, spying,
It shines on me,
Reflective.

Kyle Kilding
Boothferry Primary School

MOON

Wonderful, magical,
Flashing, dancing, sparkling,
Bright mystical glowing orbit,
Reflective.

Damon Brown (10)
Boothferry Primary School

MOON

Ghostly, white,
Spinning, sparkling, glowing,
Shining down on me,
Spherical.

Kelsea Marwood (9)
Boothferry Primary School

MOON

Beautiful, ghostly,
Dancing, sparkling, rotating,
Spinning over our heads,
Mysterious.

Laura Jackson (9)
Boothferry Primary School

SUN

Fiery, volcanic,
Flaming, boiling, blazing,
So hot you'll die,
Universal.

Ashley Young
Boothferry Primary School

SUN

Volcanic, magical,
Flashing, blazing, flaming,
Glowing, sparkling in space,
Burning.

Michelle Brooksbank
Boothferry Primary School

SUN

Bright, fiery,
Sparkling, blazing, spinning,
Flashing erupting on us,
Volcanic.

Thomas Gormley
Boothferry Primary School

SUN

Wonderful, spherical,
Burning, flashing, boiling,
Like an orange bursting,
Beautiful.

Ryan Powls
Boothferry Primary School

SUN

Gliding, floating,
Burning, boiling, blazing,
It reflects on windows,
Sparkling.

Mark Smart
Boothferry Primary School

SUN

Bright, light,
Magical, revolving, spherical,
Shining in my eyes,
Universal.

Luke Alder (9)
Boothferry Primary School

COMPASS

I know a man who's got a compass.

He found it and he followed it
        during the war.
He found it and he followed it
when he was finding his way home.
He found it and he followed it
when war was all around him.
And he followed it and he followed it
for days and days and days.

I know a man who's got a compass
and he keeps it in a box on a shelf.

It's small and white - nothing much to look at
but I think of the things he thinks
when he sees it:
how he found it
how he followed it
how he felt when war was all around him.

A small white compass
Held tight in his hand
and he keeps it in a box on a shelf
to look at now and then.

Emma Clarke & Anne-Marie Fenney
Boothferry Primary School

HANDKERCHIEF

I know a man who's got a handkerchief.

He found it and he held it
            during the war.
He found it and he held it
when he was scared.
He found it and he held it
when all was lost.
And he held it and he held it
for days and days and days.

I know a man who's got a handkerchief
and he keeps it in a box under his bed.

It's small and brown - nothing much to look at
but I think of the things he thinks
when he sees it:
how he found it
how he held it
how he felt that all was lost.

A small brown handkerchief
pushed deep in his pocket
and he keeps it in a box under his bed
to look at now and then.

Dane Powell-Guerard, Eric Wakefield & David West
Boothferry Primary School

BULLET

I know a man who's got a bullet.

He found it and he stared at it
        during the war.
He found it and he stared at it
when they were shouting for ammo.
He found it and he stared at it
when they were dying in the trenches.
And he stared at it and he stared at it
for days and days and days.

I know a man who's got a bullet
and he keeps it at the bottom of his
            wardrobe.

It's dull and grey-nothing much to look at
but I think of the things he thinks
when he sees it:
how he found it
how he stared at it
how they were shouting and dying.

A dull grey bullet
lying still by his side
and he keeps it in his wardrobe
to look at now and then.

Michael Cairns, Martyn Leek & Ashley Wood
Boothferry Primary School

GAS MASK

I know a man who's got a gas mask.

He used it and he breathed with it
                during the war.
He used it and he breathed with it
when bombs were falling.
He used it and he breathed with it
when he was dying for fresh air.
And he breathed with it and he breathed with it
          for days and days and days.

I know a man who's got a gas mask
and he keeps it in a tin behind a curtain.

It's rubbery and black - nothing much to look at
but I think of the things he thinks
when he sees it:
how he used it
how he breathed with it
how he nearly died for fresh air.

A rubbery black gas mask
fastened over his face
and he keeps it in a tin behind a curtain
to look at now and then.

Charlotte Cartwright, Annie Hollowell,
Bethany Mulley & James Wilson
Boothferry Primary School

PHOTOGRAPH

I know a woman who's got a photograph.

She was given it and she gazed at it
                during the war.
She was given it and she gazed at it
when she was crying for her love.
She was given it and she gazed at it
when her husband was long-lost.
And she gazed at it and she gazed at it
for days and days and days.

I know a woman who's got a photograph
and she keeps it in a frame on a shelf.

It's faded and brown - nothing much to look at
but I think of the things she thinks
when she sees it:
how she was given it
how she gazed at it
how she felt when she knew he was gone.

A faded brown photograph
made wet with her tears
and she keeps it in a frame on a shelf
to look at now and then.

Amy Cotton, Lauren Bolton & Samantha Hoyle
Boothferry Primary School

SIGNALLER

I know a man who's got a signaller.

He used it and he sent messages with it
        during the war.
He used it and he sent messages with it
when he was listening to the enemy.
He used it and he sent messages with it
when his country needed him.
And he sent messages with it and he sent messages with it
for days and days and days.

I know a man who's got a signaller
and he keeps it in a cupboard in his room.

It's metal and black - nothing much to look at
but I think of the things he thinks
when he sees it:
how he used it
how he sent messages with it
how he felt when his country needed him.

A metal black signaller
tapped hundreds of times
and he keeps it in a cupboard in his room
to look at now and then.

Casey Aldridge & Lauren Hughes
Boothferry Primary School

BACK TO SCHOOL

I walked to school on the first day of a new school year
Rushing and shoving in the porch
Loud gibbering and excited whispering
Pushing and speeding down the noisy corridor
Bright dazzling colours shining blindly to our eyes
The bare floor shining like an ice rink
Polished, gleaming like a star
the door was open . . .
The red bag slammers walked into the room,
We slammed our bags on the tables
as we claimed our places,
we talked to our teacher,
hearing new rules.
The girls were giggling, giggling like fools.

Class 4
Gareth Joyce (11)
Burton Agnes CE Primary School

AUTUMN

The trees are a skeleton
with brown, orange, green, crispy leaves,
bright purple plums
dropping off the trees.
Green conker shells
with conkers peeking out.
Apples ripening on the trees
red like a shiny cricket ball.
. . . The farmers scatter the seeds for next year.

Michael Hughes (9) & Luke Pickering (10)
Burton Agnes CE Primary School

Back To School

I walked to school on the first day of a new school year
Pushing and shoving in the porch,
Loud gibbering and excited whispering,
Pushing and speeding down the noisy corridor.
Bright dazzling colours shining blindly into our eyes,
The bare floor shining like an ice rink
Polished, gleaming like a star.
The door was open . . .
We gaped open mouthed,
Red bags slammed on every table
Shall I sit with him or her?
Teacher walked in;
Silence fell fast asleep in the air.
Infants shouting and screaming loud,
Tug of war starts with chairs
Clicks and clangs of legs.

Class 4
Zoe Thompson (11)
Burton Agnes CE Primary School

Referee

I watch the contestants' line,
As the group form into a triangle,
I'm trying to referee
But thoughts haunt me,
I see the crowd change into a charging rhino,
But there are a few un-biased supporters-
I hope they're supporting *Me!*

Michael Kendall (10)
Burton Agnes CE Primary School

EVERYONE'S GONE, IT'S NOT HOME TIME IS IT?

In the entrance hall
lonely fish
swimming in circles

In the staff room
Marshmallows
in cooling cocoa

In the head's office
the telephone
ringing, ringing

In the hall
no broken arms
or legs

In the classroom,
no latin,
no yawns . . .

Computers buzzing
Screensavers on
Half typed work

Everyone comes in
Oh, Oh
It was fire drill.

James Foster (10)
Burton Agnes CE Primary School

WHERE'S EVERYBODY?

In the cafeteria,
abandoned pots
taps left dripping.

In the computer room
computer left running
curtains flapping.

In the library
books flipping open
ornaments knocked over.

In the nursery playground
leaves still blowing
branches swaying steadily.

Deserted pencil cases
stone cold
papers blowing through windows,

but out in the playground
the fire drill
goes on . . .

Cheyenne Tebbett (9)
Burton Agnes CE Primary School

MY DREAM

I went in a rocket to a far away land
It was big and round and covered with sand
I went for a walk my rocket took off
And left me there for years.

Natalie Hodgson (10)
Cowick CE Primary School

RAIN

Pitter, patter, oh I'm bored,
I decided to draw,
But the activity isn't enough,
I go outside, my boots are already wet through.
I come in, I sit next to the windowpane,
The weather vane,
Goes haywire.
Drum, Drum!
If I go out, people will think I'm dumb.
Plop, plop!
The raindrops drop.
Oh what a boring day.
Nothing to do, I want to play.
I can't though, oh what a pity,
This flooded city.
Oh, when will it stop raining?
My face keeps draining.
Of colour.

Daniel Andrews (10)
Cowick CE Primary School

RAIN

Pitter, patter goes the rain,
On our roof what a horrible day.
I'm really, really, bored!
Nothing to do, nothing to play.

Drip, drip down the drain.
It's like I'm in a bath,
With all the water around me.
All the puddles on the path.

Kieron Waterson (10)
Cowick CE Primary School

THE CAT

As she ventures through the leaves
Searching for her tea
She weaves her way through the tangled branches
As quiet as can be
Twisting
Turning
Dodging
Diving
She carries on searching
For her prey
Over crunching branches
Where they lay.

Louisa Cooke (10)
Cowick CE Primary School

DOG

My dog went for a jog
And while he was jogging
He found a log
Then he found another dog,
They ran off together
Then they were all alone
The owners had gone home.

Bianca Kirsopp (10)
Cowick CE Primary School

RAIN

Thud, Thud hear the rain
Bouncing on the ground
Thud, Thud hear the rain.
Trickling down the stream
Thud, Thud hear the rain
Pouring down the tent
Thud, Thud hear the rain
Splashing on the window sill
Oh when will the rain stop
Please, Please, Please stop.

Samantha Best (10)
Cowick CE Primary School

RAIN

The drumming of the rain
Oh what a pain
I want to go outside and play football in the rain.
The pitch is all boggy,
I don't know what to do.
The rain is still lashing against the window pane
Rain is so boring,
Rain, rain, rain.

Rachael Deighton (10)
Cowick CE Primary School

RAIN

Pitter. patter
It's raining, it's raining,
What an awful day!
It's raining, it's raining,
I'm so bored.
There's nothing to do.
It's raining, it's raining.
I hate it when it rains,
It's such a pain,
It's boring when it rains,
There's nothing to play.

Nathan Redford (11)
Cowick CE Primary School

RAIN

Rain, rain what a pain
Overflowing in the drain
Seeping back into river
Putting floodbanks at full strain
Boom!
Mud flies cows scatter
Water fills the Gowdall Ings
Oh no! The houses.

James Duffin (10)
Cowick CE Primary School

Rainy Day

When the falls on my window it makes noises
When I'm in bed I can hear it loud and fast
When it stops the noise is past.
I like to play out in the rain
With my bat and skipping rope
Rain leaves behind lots of puddles
Little children stand talking in huddles.
My mum hates it when it rains
My brother cannot go out and play
Clothes hang wet on the washing line
Soon the rain stops. I like it fine.

Carolanne Turner (10)
Cowick CE Primary School

Rain

It's a rainy day today,
Oh! I want to go and play.
I'm doing something boring
And I'm going to start snoring.
Pitter-patter goes the rain,
The continuous drumming is such a pain.
I've got to stay awake,
While I watch the growing lake.

Kelly Heard (11)
Cowick CE Primary School

THE ACE SPACE RACE

Three, the engines roared.
Two, the rockets sang.
One, pilots got on board.
Zero, the space race began.
Eleven was in the lead.
Four close behind.
Two and three both lost their speed.
They were both left behind.
Six used turbo speed.
He bravely took the lead.
But not without a challenge.
Eleven shot him down.
A mile from the finishing line.
Eleven thought it was fine.
But to his despair he'd lost right there.
For four had gone over the line.

John Kirk (11)
Cowick CE Primary School

RAIN

My friends and I were in a tent,
The rain came torrenting down.
We listened as it went pitter patter,
Pitter-patter on the sides of our little
                        green tent.
We all slid under our sleeping bags and
All of a sudden it stopped!
We all jumped up from under the covers,
And happily shouted 'Hooray!'

Rebecca Cooke (10)
Cowick CE Primary School

THE RAIN

The rain patting on the path
The river flows slowly in the moonlight
The leaves float off the tree
The rain taps on the door step
The rain dripped into the stream.

I watched the rain go down the drain
What a boring day.

Emma Wales (10)
Cowick CE Primary School

MEMORY LANE

As I lay awake at night
while others are asleep
I take a trip down Memory Lane
With tears upon my cheeks.

No one knows the heartache
I've tried so hard to hide
No one knows how many times
I've broken down and cried.

Cried because I love you
cried because I cared
And cried because when I wake up
I know you won't be there.

So please believe me
I won't be sad or blue
All I will do
Is remember how much I love you.

Rebecca Lawtey (10)
East Halton Primary School

GROWING UP

When I was one
I sucked my thumb.

When I was two
I was brand new.

When I was three
I had no friends but me.

When I was four
I knocked at the door.

When I was five
I was high.

When I was six
I picked up sticks.

When I was seven
I went to visit heaven.

When I was eight
I had a cool mate.

When I was nine
I drank wine.

When I was ten
I visited the hen.

When I was eleven
I was clever as ever!

Kellie North (11)
East Halton Primary School

WINTER

I woke to a winter morning
It was a cold one too
There was Jack Frost on the window
And some snow outside too.

The snow was white and fluffy
And sparkled in the sun
The tree branches are all shiny
With little red berries peeping through.

Birds were hopping through the snow
Rabbits bouncing in it too.
Foxes are leaving their footprints
But the big bold footprints are mine

Cold icicles hang on the window ledge
Glistening in the sun
They slowly began to melt away
Drip, drip - until they had all gone.

Rebecca Turner (9)
East Halton Primary School

ORANGE

Fast, violent flames floating on a huge ball;
It spits and spurts ready to fall,
It heats us up when we are cold,
It begins to spit and scold.

The sun has gone in it begins to chill,
It comes out again and begins to kill.
A fire has begun
People are coming by the ton.

Hazel Newton (11)
East Halton Primary School

LOVE

Love is wrong
Love can be strong.
Love is everything but long.

Love is right
Love's a fight
Love is like a flickering light.

Love is right
Love is wrong
Love is like a rollercoaster ride.

Love is pink
Love's like a wink
Love is very very weak.

Love is right, love is wrong
Love is anything you want even long.

Denise Parker (11)
East Halton Primary School

GREEN

The grass is shining through the light
As an ant is devoured by a termite.
She stares; longingly through the trees,
Whilst there's a rustling of the leaves.

As she stares up to the sky,
The leaves suddenly begin to fly.
They float up, up and away,
But they'll be back another day.

Adam Rowbotham (11)
East Halton Primary School

THE SWALLOW

Swift swift the swallow flies,
Swift swift the swallow is wise.

Swift swift as black as coal,
Swift swift as blind as a mole.

Swift swift as nice as wine,
Swift swift as thin as a vine.

Swift swift as quiet as a bee
Swift swift as smart as me.

Holly Evans (11)
East Halton Primary School

MY DOG

I own a poozee
Known to all just as Suzie.
She's something quite unique
for she moves with perfection on her feet
She enjoys a lot to eat
Especially at shows it must be a treat
She really can almost talk
Especially when I say 'walk Suzie walk
If I had one wish to make
It would be for Suzie to be my playmate.

Emma Turner (10)
East Halton Primary School

RAIN TO PUDDLE!

Rain drumming, belting down,
Glaring at the world.
Misty pearls, falling in a dash,
Crystal clean!
Still!
As it hits the ground,
Puddle!
Changing
Into a beer brown of churned up mud.
A ripple of sound,
Rushing through as rain turns to puddle.
Still staying like pale dishwater.
Rain!

Rachael Schofield (11)
Hornsea CP School

PARENTS' EVENING

Sitting down nervously
Silence passed over.
Impulsive panic overpowered me.
Wondering . . . dreaming.
As I twirled my fingers aggressively
A sigh like a long whisper filled the room.
Tick, tock, tick, tock.
Over soon,
Over soon . . .
Waiting, tense.
Expecting, hoping.

Kirsthy McNaughton (11)
Hornsea CP School

THE JOURNEY OF THE STORM

The fiery sun,
Hung like a lemon
In the blue sky.

While I'm sitting at my desk,
Working!
I look out of the window,
The sun was gone.

Thick, inky black clouds
Filled the sky.
The first rain spat on the window,
Lightning!
The lights flicker.

And then it was over,
The fiery sun,
Hung like a lemon,
In the blue sky.

Louise Pannhausen (10)
Hornsea CP School

EARTH

Earth turned dark,
Absolute blackness.
Rats roaming
Moving through chaos.
Fumes rising,
Buildings crumbling!
Our earth is shattered.
Journey ended . . .
Silence.

James Varley (11)
Hornsea CP School

JOURNEY INTO SPACE!

I saw a flying saucer while driving in my Corsa,
I got out to take a look, and looked it up in my alien book.
It came down and shone a light and took me up in the
darkest night.
So here I am trapped and lost,
whatever it is whatever the cost,
I'm gonna get out of here no matter what.
I'm in the Captain's cabin,
no aliens around,
got to steer this thing home safely on the ground.
I've found a swirling vortex to take me home,
Oh dear I've landed on the Millennium Dome!

Jessica Cox (11)
Hornsea CP School

MY TRIP TO SCOTLAND

I went to Scotland with my mum.
I had lots of fun.
I went in a car.
It was far.
It was pouring with rain.
It ran down the drain.
We stayed in a caravan.
The sun came out and I got a tan.

Bryony Cox (11)
Hornsea CP School

A JOURNEY TO HEAVEN

See the doves fly above you,
As you walk the stairs to heaven,
You see the angels pass you by,
Smiling gratefully.

You see the devil going down,
Trying to climb the stairs,
He's never going to get up,
Because he disobeyed.

You've reached three doors,
Which one do you take?
Say a prayer . . .

Dear God,
     Please help me choose the right door, because I want to live with
your son in heaven. Amen. He answers . . .
He says 2nd . . . You take it. Now your Holy Spirit shall *Live 4eva.*

Natalie Wardill (10)
Hornsea CP School

GOING UNDER THE SEA

Fishes fishes under the sea
Eating weeds for their tea
Fishes fishes over there
They are everywhere.
Fishes fishes under the sea
Going round and round
Messing up the ground
They saw a tadpole swimming
The shark came up chasing the
                          woman.

Samantha Chew (10)
Hornsea CP School

SHOOTING STAR

Shooting star,
Clear away the rainy clouds.
In the blue sky,
Please shoot them away.

Shooting star,
Come back soon.
From your Planet,
In the sky.

Shooting star,
Through the blue and misty sky,
We hope to see you soon.

Shooting star,
Shoot so far away in the sky.
Your journey will soon come to an end,
Shooting through the sky.

Darryl Eastwood (10)
Hornsea CP School

RAINDROP

Crystal beads dropping
Bursting with life.
Glittering with silver beams
Falling, drifting gently
To new precious earth.
Life arrives
In small beaded drops
For thirsty creatures
To lap up.

Adam Whitaker (11)
Hornsea CP School

SHOOTING STAR

I don't know, but I wonder why,
How stars shoot through the sky.
I think it's wonderful, Don't you,
How they dance about in navy blue.
They always seem to have their way,
And a new one comes up every day.

      In the night you shoot so beautiful and bright,
      I'm the luckiest person because you are in my sight.
      In the night you zoom around the sun and moon,
      Then you loop d loop and say you'll come back soon.
      On your voyage you fly so far,
      Well. That's a bit silly cause you are a star.

You fly,
You shoot,
You loop d loop,
You do what normal stars can.
You jump up high, but never die,
And do what you want without a plan.

Charlotte Empsall (10)
Hornsea CP School

VOYAGE

Cruel moan of the menacing darkness,
Stroking down the wavy chute.
Bank collapsing into dashing gloom! . . .
Boats overturned by the lurking strength of the shivery blackness,
Creatures cramped onto sharp edges.
Wide opening stretching,
Spreading out like ink blocks.

Luke Naylor (10)
Hornsea CP School

JOURNEY OUT OF BED

This is how I woke up from my favourite place on land,
First I flickered my hazel eyes and
Wiped them with my hand.
Then I slightly moved my foot till it touched the ground.
Then all of a sudden I heard a sound,
Oh it was only my miserable hound.
Then my mum brought up some pies
For me and her,
To share.
So then I moved my helpless arm until it was standing tall.
Then I heard the old man who owns the market stall,
So that's what I heard in my favourite place on land.

Shaun Brooke (10)
Hornsea CP School

WATER CYCLE

Trickling through tiny cheeks
Mud and grime
Rushing like an angry wolf.
Hissing, squirming,
Running, rushing,
Will it never end?
Invisible force . . . upwards never to stop
To a family in the sky.
Struggling like trapped fishes
Lurking in the sky.
Shrieking as it smashes to the ground
Like a never ending train ride.

Michael Smith (10)
Hornsea CP School

PARENTS' EVENING

Ticking like a bomb
Waiting to explode.
4 o'clock . . .
Door swinging
Creaking like old bones
Slamming shut.
4.05 . . .
Sitting thinking
Positive?
Negative?
4.10 . . .
Blood rushing
Like a steam train.
Hot
Sweaty.
4.15 . . .
Relief
Relax
All over!
4.20 . . .

Ben Asquith (11)
Hornsea CP School

MY DAY TRIP

I went to Flamingo Land for the day
I went a long way
I went on a fast ride
My mum was by my side
I had lots to eat
I had very tired feet.

Alannah Colley (10)
Hornsea CP School

MY TRIP TO WALES

I went to Wales
I heard some tales
About some mountains
I went on outings
I saw the sea
I got chased by a bee
I went around the castle
I caused lots of hassle
My mum had a fit
I had a sulk for a bit
I went to Wales
The boats had sails
There was no dome
I'm glad to be home.

Ashley Evans (10)
Hornsea CP School

VOLCANO

Bursting like a balloon
Over the full shone moon.
Splittering, splurting, molten lava
Trickles down like burning treacle.
Like a snake swallowing rats
Crashing buildings in its path
Until . . .
It fades and fades
Till rock remains
Completing its devastation.

Kerry Railton (10)
Hornsea CP School

Journey To The Sky

In the hot fire, flames flare.
In the sky the fireworks glare,
The sky is filled
with whistling
sparks,
People hurrying
to watch the
fireworks,
I saw
a beautiful
rocket fly
It whizzed through
the dark sky.

Katie Russell (10)
Hornsea CP School

Voyages

Spitting from the dark sky . . .
Colours intense,
Bright red as blood.
Twisting and plunging to the ground.
Wrapping round.
Whirling down.
Lashing like angry whips.
Twirling to the earth.

Anna-May Rogers (10)
Hornsea CP School

DESERT JOURNEY

Blustering winds blow around
I wrap in my garment on the ground.
Sounds in the wind give me fright
I have to stay there all night.

The winds have dropped, I took my chance
In front of me a sun reflected glance.
I carried on with hope and fear
Will an oasis suddenly appear.

The sun shone bright
The dunes stand tall in height
Sand whispers cutting like a knife.

Stuttering amongst the twilight
The oasis is coming clear
I attempt to keep cool
Looking, seeking for any food.

Louis Lawson (11)
Hornsea CP School

THE CRICKET JOURNEY

Expectation clogged the stadium.
The players bustle out.
Thrill wraps them like a blanket.
Their spikes churn the square
And the umpire hobbles on.
Time slithers away.
Donald, in like a steam train.
Rips through teams
And the series is won.

Ben Wallis (10)
Hornsea CP School

PARENTS' EVENING

(Passing Time)
Strange thoughts.
Worried.
Sweaty palm,
Fidgeting feet,
Shuffling chairs,
Nervous twitches,
Muffled voices,
Tinkling laughs . . .
Familiar faces,
Smirking smiles,
Sigh,
It's passed.

Kate Southey (11)
Hornsea CP School

ANGER

Rough - red colour ran round me
Spinning through my mind.
Lurking right behind me.
Hot tears like burning oil.
Steaming, stamping, dark and gloomy.
Like hot lava flowing.
Lashes of whip splattered red in front of me.
Frowning, scowling,
Winced with a long sigh . . .

Katie Robinson (10)
Hornsea CP School

VOYAGES

Blackness, devastating the world.
Derelict,
Industrial buildings, belching, belching
Toxic waste.
World, dead as a corpse.
Wind sighed, like a long whisper.
Churned up oil,
Sliding across a changed world,
Like rivers of blood.
Rotting, reeking.
Animals - No more!
People - No more!
The world - No more . . .

Chris Hawksworth (11)
Hornsea CP School

WATER

Undercurrent of laughter,
Eyes ablaze,
Danger Struck!
Speedier than ever,
My thoughts overpowered me.
Dark clammy sky,
Calm returned,
Fear came racing in my head.

Jayne Girling (10)
Hornsea CP School

VOYAGES

Shattered plates for protection.
Green glass for decoration.
Heated liquid for food!
Bones covered in mud for arms.
Green confetti for hair!
Insisting on standing tall.
Frozen water far inside.
Hollow, no more is its trunk.
Powerful - a perfect treasure.
Bursting with life.

Michael Prescott (10)
Hornsea CP School

DARKNESS

A ripple of horror
Passing over me.
A blanket of darkness
Surges down,
Covering secrets
With a deathly silence.
Lights like pin pricks
On a velvety black curtain.
Deeper, deeper,
Until all is shrouded
In blackness.

Natalie Wilson (10)
Hornsea CP School

THE HOCKEY JOURNEY

Air clogged with cold.
Heart pounding like a machine.
Nervous.
Sweat puddling on my forehead.
Silence.
A whistle,
A tackle,
A goal,
A victory,
At home,
On the couch,
In the silence,
I was proud.

Ben Cheer (10)
Hornsea CP School

DREAMY JOURNEY

I went to space in an aeroplane
And guess what I saw:
A monkey's head on a rabbit's bed.

A six foot bear on an infant chair.
A moose with a goose.

Then to my surprise
I saw the sun rise.

Morning

Ashleigh Bray (10)
Hornsea CP School

TIME VOYAGES

Dead or alive, time never stands still.
Changing - slow to fast,
Stopping at every number
Time flicks all the hours away.

Slowly it passes by
Some notice it, some don't.
Time will never end.
As it trickles past
It ticks away its life
'Til the time of death.

Shaun Taylor (10)
Hornsea CP School

NATURE AND LIFE

Clear spits climbing down,
Kind light shone,
Everything changed.
Sigh like a long whisper.
Trees like curly wire,
Stretching their fingers like flames
Clutching every leaf.
Magic lurks everywhere.
Colours stream along the sky.
Mother nature is content.

Kayleigh Hampson (10)
Hornsea CP School

THE JOURNEY OF SEED TO TREE

The sycamore helicopter,
Had spiralled to the ground,
Burrowed into the damp dark earth,
And waited.
The soil closed around it like a blanket
Roots.
Shoots.
A tree.
Thick inky masses of apple green leaves,
Green moss massaged the bark.
Then crumbles in death.

Alec Tomlinson (11)
Hornsea CP School

THE JOURNEY OF THE FOOTBALL MATCH

The air chilled,
Frozen.
Grass stiff with frost.
My boots punched holes through frozen leaves.
A mass of dark cloud billowed overhead
Menacing.
Fear flooded the field.
The whistle blew.
The game begins
The journey has begun.

Daniel Roberts (10)
Hornsea CP School

THE JOURNEY OF STRANGE THINGS!

I was running down the street,
and fell over some feet.
On to my double boned knee,
and what did I see?
I saw a:
Moose jump over a Goose.
I saw a:
Cat with an extraordinary!
I saw a:
Mum who was plump,
and a baby with a bump
Then I decided to leg it
but . . . (Crash, bang) I fell down a pit!

Frances M Hackett (11)
Hornsea CP School

THE TESTING JOURNEY

A furious red sun,
Sizzled the back of his neck,
A world of secrecy lay in front of him.
A breath of nervousness swept over him.
A test paper.
It lay like an ordinary object
But it hid such horrors.

Silence flooded the room.
He daydreamed
Of sparkling springs
And summer sunshine . . .

Michael Bradley (10)
Hornsea CP School

RIDING THROUGH THE NIGHT

One dark and damp and eerie night,
When I was full of fright,
I was on a journey,
and it was scary,
Riding through the night.

I rode further in the dark,
When suddenly from across the park,
There was a light and it was green!
Who could it have been?
Riding through the night.

Then at high speed I fled,
Up the lane as fast as I could, I sped,
Then a cry came from down the lane,
It sounded like a cry of pain,
Riding through the night.

Thomas Read (11)
Hornsea CP School

NIGHT RUN

Tiger running through the night,
past the trees and eerie light,
running fast with all his might,
overwhelmed with mist and fright.

Shooting past
to his mother's call,
Stumbling but didn't fall,
nearly there there's not a care
for him except his mother.

Snuggled up on the ground,
Concealed within his mother's arms,
this is where he likes to be,
Safe outside the hollow tree.

Catherine Suret (11)
Hornsea CP School

THE JOURNEY

Whistling through the trees,
Gallop, Gallop.
Swiftly, swerving in and out.

Hooves clashing
Whips lashing
Over the stile
Wait for it . . . *Splash!*
In the water,
Up and off again.

Round the bend
And on the straight
Jump over the hedge
Whip whip
Gallop gallop.

Next lap
Here we go again . . .
Splash!
Faster, faster.
    Finish.

Aaron Scott (10)
Hornsea CP School

Rain

Gazing down on the world,
Like a misty pearl,
Swifter, swifter . . .
Swifter than the speed of light!
Like stars on a clear silver night.
A splash . . . a faint gentle splash,
Clear drops like royal rings,
Zooming, zooming down!
The snaky route it takes
It skimmed on the water,
Over, all over, at last . . .

Hollie Parnham Stevens (11)
Hornsea CP School

Voyages

Whirls and strikes down the river banks,
Punches doors open,
As if it's in its strongest power.
Darting and squeezing between buildings,
Jolting and jerking around
Deep flooded cellars.
Sinks into the flow of the river
Where the ripples in the water swirl.

Chris Nicholson (10)
Hornsea CP School

THE JOURNEY OF BOREDOM

Wake up, wake up my mother said.
Haul your body out of bed.
The day is new the sun is out,
Get out of bed you lazy lout.
Unwillingly I rise and shine,
Hip Hip hooray, the day is mine.
Shredded wheat or wheetabix,
All the same . . . like eating sticks.
My mum suggests a trip to the zoo,
I bet she thinks that I'm still two.
The museum trip was pretty lame,
It's a boring fogies hall of fame.
A picnic lunch out on the grass,
When something nasty bites my . . . bum.
We're going back home on the bus,
I don't start a row 'cos I can't stand the fuss.
The conductor surveys me with beady eyes,
They remind me gran's mince pies.
These chips taste like a gravel drive,
It's a wonder how I can stay alive.
'You have to learn to educate,'
'C ya mum I'm off to my mate's.'
I need to rest my sleepy head,
I'm glad to be back in my bed.
Aaaaaahhhhhh! Bliss!

Tom Prout (10)
Hornsea CP School

JOURNEY THROUGH THE AMAZON

I'm burning,
Hot and fiery is my name,
Volcanoes bow below my feet,
For I am Goddess of the Sun,
On my journey through the Amazon.

Quickly travelling,
Fires revive,
The forest is burning,
The river beds dry,
The Amazon is burning,
All because of my flames.

The forest is golden, shimmering bright,
My heart is pumping proud,
Blood rushes toward my fingers,
My last flame of victory emerges,
The Amazon is flaming.

Forest fire burn and rush,
The Amazon is ablaze,
My journey is finally over,
My fire completed,
The Amazon is no more!

Michaela Armstrong (11)
Hornsea CP School

THE VOYAGE OF THE FUTURE

It lay dead, silent on the sand, immobiled to the ground,
always moved so rough or soft but once again is found.
In peace and harmony it will lie,
Waiting for the time,
to dance along the ocean blue,
to impart its message clue.
The sandy shore will break the tide,
While the message will hide,
amongst the rubble of waves.

A crown of waves crowding around,
the message of no sound,
that bobs along the foamy feathers,
always alone and wondering whether
the time will come,
when the voyage is done.
The bottle keeps finding,
The bottle keeps hiding
amongst the rubble of waves.

On the horizon land is spied,
amongst pebbles the message nestles and hides.
The darkness thickens while pushing the message towards
its destination within rock hoards.
Giant fronds shade the dusty sand.
Someone's future lies in front of a bony hand.
The message stops finding,
The message stops hiding,
amongst the rubble of waves.

Amanda Ashburner (11)
Hornsea CP School

JOURNEY TO THE CLOUDS

Up up she rose,
Given God's gift to the clouds.
She grew bigger.
A spiral spike,
Emerging through her head.
Her skin was sprouting hairs.
Wings spreading from her back,
Hands and feet swapped for hooves,
Gold and bright.
Her hair taken away, a mane to cover
for it.
Creeping through at the back, a tail.
Her journey was over, fully evolved into
a unicorn.

She has now got the speed to push the
clouds across the sky,
Her pointed spike acting like a lightning
conductor.
Her body helping to bring light to the world.
Her hooves shining like the sun,
Every step brings beams of light to earth.
She really was God's new birth.

Sarah-Louise Gardener (10)
Hornsea CP School

CAMEL KING

I am a king from lands afar
On a camel following a star.

So far it's led me to Bethlehem
Where I see Mary and Joseph then.

> Then I see a baby sweet
> I wonder if it wants something to eat.
>
> I wonder why, I wonder how
> then I see a pig and a cow.

I would be able to give you my gift
If only this stupid cow would shift.

When we gave it we bent on one knee
Only to find it's the wrong baby.

> It is a long time on the way back
> Especially when your camel has a water lack
>
> 'Hey guys Summat new to learn
> We've just took a mega wrong turn.'

I think that we're in France
then some flamenco lady starts to dance.

I've just found out that we're in Spain
Orrrhh I'm not going through that again.

Edward Naylor (10)
Hornsea CP School

JOURNEY TO THE SKY

Up, up and away I go,
to the south for winter,
I wonder where that is?
My mum says stay beside her,
but she flies too fast for me,
I wonder why it's called the south?
For me and you it's a mystery!

Up, up and away I go,
to the south for winter.
There's my mate Bill,
he must be going to the same place as me.
Where is my mum,
has she left me?
Everyone gone for ever.
Oh no they're not.
I'm in front of them.

Up, up and away I go,
to the south for winter.
Oh my goodness I've fallen,
Mum . . .
I'm back again,
I'm on a journey of flight,
help me my wings are tired,
I'm falling asleep,
we're there, the journey is finished.
Yes it's time to sleep.

Kelsie Wason (11)
Hornsea CP School

The Fallen Angel's Resurrection

Golden wings pierce the darkness,
Flowing silver journeys the sky,
Golden hoop, the sacred halo,
As up, up. up she fly.

Golden heart, a light so bright
White hair, a startling sight,
As her great God, high on top,
Calls her up to the heavens above.

Her glowing wings spread apart,
A quickened beating is about to start.
The heavenly air about her fair,
From the Earth, she is about to depart.

The rushing air cold and frozen,
Leaping high, her feet go,
As she rises upwards, up she go,
Her journey to the heavens has just begun.

Flapping swiftly, flying upwards,
The heavens coming ever nearer,
No more standing at death's door,
The blackened evil gone from her.

The dragon's wings that once were hers,
The evil heart that consumed the good,
No more, all gone, for she is resurrected,
As her pale skin touches the heavens above.

Her journey once begun,
Took a month, and a day to be done,
But now her evil heart has gone,
She joins the Lord, her heavenly God.

Kirsty Peck (11)
Hornsea CP School

MY DIARY FROM
'MY JOURNEY THROUGH UTOPIA'

As I travelled through the land
I expected to find some surf and sand
Here with the wackiest, weirdest things
This is where my adventure begins!

First there was sherbet
Deep fried in fat
Also the lollies
That flatten you. *Splat!*

The Ferraris they sold
Were ten pennies each
Sold on miles
Of white, sandy beach.

The glue they made
Was super sticky
It also smelt
A wee bit icky.

But then I saw
a rescue plane
to take me
safely home again.

And then half home
I see, what's that
It is the monster
I squashed flat.

I toss maltesers, two, three,
But still it wants to pursue me
Out I drop my catalytic converter
Onto the monster's head, to hurt 'er.

Phil Taylor (11)
Hornsea CP School

FOOTBALL

Footballers running up the pitch,
Offside in the area,
Opponents sweating because of pressure,
Time running out for a goal,
Ball flying through the air,
At the edge of the area, he shoots
                      and scores,
Lovely goal everybody shouts as he passes,
Last the full time whistle blows!

Peter Jones (9)
Kingsway Primary School

MY PRECIOUS BOX

I would put in my precious box
My new red motorbike
and my good friend Mike
Who likes my bike.

My red patterned helmet and
my superstar trousers
all as shiny as steel
with my motorbike shoes
As blue as the sky.

Dale Malcolmson (10)
Kingsway Primary School

In My Special Box I Will Put . . .

In my special box I will put . . .
the common green,
the growth of a runner bean,
the sparkle on the river and of course
the breeze's quiver.

In my special box I will put . . .
the friendship of my friends,
whereabouts the road bends,
the world of books and the turn of . . .
brooks.

In my special box I will put . . .
the silence of night,
the beauty of light,
the joy of everyday life and
my personal life.

In my special box I will put . . .
a silent class,
my treasured glass,
my 'for life' teddy and
my nice big bed.

Sian Hastings (9)
Kingsway Primary School

Babys

B   abies calling for their dummy.
A   nd asking for their toys.
B   abies screaming,
Y   elling loudly,
S   o everyone can hear.

Natalie Wreakes (9)
Kingsway Primary School

THE MAGIC WATERFALL GARDEN

Running, leaping, sprinting with joy I run through the gardens,
My dress trailing through the flowers, a blue paradise.
Sparkling purples, blues, golden flowers glint in the sun.
I ran along, I looked down, there was a big waterfall below.
I went down to the waterfall and looked at the weeds,
that looked like they were grabbing the other pebbles and reeds.
I love the way it rushes by as I put my feet in the water,
They feel the freshness of its minty coolness.
I put on my socks and shoes and pass round the bend,
I saw the goldfish that I bought all swimming . . . all made friends.
I love the way the water flows among the rocks and stones.
The freshness of the days sweeping along as I voyage through
                                                    my garden.

April Boyes (8)
North Frodingham Primary School

SPACE VOYAGE

I feel scared and nervous
I wriggle in my seat
Countdown begins.
The engine grumbles and shatters
A sudden blast
I shake my body rigid
Outside the window I see a blur
Then blackness and stars appear.
I hear myself speaking
I am amazed
My journey begins.

David Edwards (7)
North Frodingham Primary School

MY MAGIC FLYING UNICORN

My magic flying unicorn galloping in a moonlit sky.
We go on a journey so I hold tight because we're really high.
We play with the stars and go to sleep on the moon.
And play in the morning with the comets till noon.
Now you know this is where we play
Now I am saying I don't want to go away.
We stay here and stay here and say it's a home
And I brush my hair with a star not a comb.
I cuddle the stars, comets and moon,
And say 'goodbye I'll see you soon.'

So me and my unicorn turn back to our voyage.

Soon I start missing the stars, comet and moon
I really want to live there not just for the noon.
Now I'm going to start the voyage back
I've packed my luggage in a sack
As soon as I get there I give them a cuddle
Now I know I'm not going to be in a muddle.

And soon I'm the moon's family.

Anne-Marie Edwards (9)
North Frodingham Primary School

IMAGINE BEING A DRAGON

Imagine being a dragon living in a cave.
Imagine being a dragon ruling the earth.
My flames burn trees to ash.
My fire is as hot as the sun.
My eyes are light as gold.

Hollie Warren (8)
North Frodingham Primary School

OWLS

I flutter across the skies with golden wings spread.
Quickly swooping down to the ground for a big plump
                                                    mouse.
Up with a flash to my babies in a nest
Cheeping and flapping, as I come with their meal.
I rest my eyes and warm my babies, my new life starts,
The golden shiny sun is bright and warm.
I can get out to spread my wings from my crowded home.
My babies start flying with me in the endless skies,
We spot some worms creeping around.
I swooped down and grabbed them and return to my nest
                                            to rest my body.
With a thump I woke.
At once I see what is the matter.
There sitting on my windowsill was a lovely owl.

Jane Howey (8)
North Frodingham Primary School

THE MIDNIGHT FLIGHT

As I fly through the dark misty sky
Stars are gleaming like diamonds.
The sea is sparkling like sapphire
The wind is turning a soft gentle breeze
Grass is as green as an emerald.
Leaves are as red as a ruby as they toss gently
Across the land.

Matthew Rymaruk (8)
North Frodingham Primary School

THE OLD HOUSE

Across the road
an old house lies.
Nobody inside
I usually pass by.
Today I feel drawn inside.
With torch and bag
I creep inside.
The metal gates squeak out loud
Nobody hears.
The old gravelled drive
crunches under my feet.
I open the door and there
on the wall a picture lies
It seems to be following me around
I hear a noise, a moan and groan
Then the phone, a creak, a scream, a shout.
It sent a shiver down my spine.
I ran out yowling in the dark, I run inside.
And it's by itself again and I only pass by.

Corey Wylie (8)
North Frodingham Primary School

THE FLYING MAT

My flying mat goes swiftly through the bright golden sky.
I see the people that look like specks of dust.
I see the houses they look like bricks
I see the brilliant view of green, yellow and golden brown.
I see people bathing in rivers
I see homeless people in bins
My house is there, let's land.

Joseph Copeland (9)
North Frodingham Primary School

TRAVELLING THROUGH THE DESERT

Travelling through the desert in the summerlit sky
On a lumpy camel where the eagles fly.
Hot and boiling, no water to see.
No one to go with just the camel and me.
Travelling through the desert where the sand
                         drifts away,
Nowhere to stop, nowhere to stay.
I don't know how, I don't know when,
I don't know if I'll see my parents again.
But still I wait, travelling alone.
If only I could find me a home.
I can see a dry desert, a scene.
I wake up . . . it's only a dream.
My dreams take me to distant lands,
Like the one I've just had covered in sand.
It seems like the dreams are true,
I thought it was.
I wonder.
Did you? . . .

Claire Edwards (9)
North Frodingham Primary School

MAGIC CARPET

My magic carpet goes flying
Over the mountains across the seas,
to a place called India.
I see people homeless
no food to eat,
no water to drink,
So I turn back home
Very sad.

Korina Cullen (8)
North Frodingham Primary School

THE MAGIC SEABIRD

Swooping, gliding through the sky
Looking down with golden eyes.
Looking down on the sparkling sea
Making sure her eyes are safe on
The cliff edge below.
Golden eggs and golden wings
At night she rests.
Then soon when tomorrow comes
The eggs begin to crack.
A little head pops out of its egg
As the beautiful seabird with wind through
                              her feathers
And she glides through the clear blue sky
Above.

Hannah Harewood (8)
North Frodingham Primary School

A VOYAGE BACK IN TIME

I voyage through time
in my car and see the past
Stegosaurus stomping around
Tyrannosaurus trampling the ground
Pterodactyl swooping down
Last of dark green forests.
I explore swamps and lakes
I see some gigantasaurus
killing for food
I search for the way home.

James Pearson (7)
North Frodingham Primary School

UP IN SPACE

V ery scared up in space
O n my own about to feel sick
Y esterday I was on the ground
A nd now I'm about to faint.
G oing into a black hole.
E verything seems so weird.

Daniel Charlton (9)
North Frodingham Primary School

VOYAGES OVER SEA

Voyages over sea
Wonder when we go home
Nothing yummy to eat
All this sea makes me sick
No garden or house
I wish I was home again.

Jenny Howey (9)
North Frodingham Primary School

A VOYAGE ACROSS THE SEA

V oyage ahead
O ver the old sea
Y awning all day long
A nother day of deep blue sea
G oing to be here for a while
E very night and every day.

Courtney Lamb (9)
North Frodingham Primary School

RIDE ACROSS THE SKY

V oyage across the sky,
O ver the moon and over the earth,
Y ards of sky to travel through,
A sky full of stars,
G liding down the midnight air,
E arth is small from where I stare.

Thomas Pearson (9)
North Frodingham Primary School

OVER THE SEAS AND THROUGH THE FORESTS

Every day I go on a voyage
Over the seas and through the forests
As I wake up I yawn,
Night after night I dream,
About going on a voyage,
Will they ever come true.

Laura Wilson (10)
North Frodingham Primary School

VOYAGE

I Voyage through my mind
lOng ago I see all the memories.
tYpes of pleasant memories I see,
sAd memories are seen.
aGed from birth to now.
lEarning all the time.

James Doyle (10)
North Frodingham Primary School

SPACESHUTTLE 3

V oyages through space are pretty boring, really it is.
O nly some men in a rocket visiting the moon daily.
Y ou and me think it is so cool being bitten by
A liens and thrown in a lava pool
G alaxies glide gloom through the sky
E very day I see a planet looking at me.

Adam Lamb (10)
North Frodingham Primary School

VOYAGE

V egetable and fruit are so sweet.
O nions are so tangy and strong.
Y ou must eat all your tea because it makes you grow.
A pples are scrumptious.
G rapefruit is OK but my mum thinks it is very nice.
E ggplant is very unusual.

Lucy Garton (11)
North Frodingham Primary School

MY PEN

Every day my pen writes
Over and over now my ink is getting low
Yet again I start to write.
But then again I write through the night.
Gripping my pen very tight.
Even though I am asleep I still go on and write
                                    and write.

Russell Wylie (9)
North Frodingham Primary School

A FROSTY MORNING

It's very cold in the morning frosty and misty.
Over near the hills the glistening stream is frozen.
The yellow and brown leaves are speckled with white
                                        delicate frost.
All the people wrapped up warm, steam comes out of their
                                        mouths when they talk.
Grass covered in white, and sparkles like diamonds.
Everybody's cheeks are rosy red and hands and feet are frozen.
Snowflakes start falling to the ground,
        It's snowing! It's winter!

Rachel Spence (11)
North Frodingham Primary School

VOYAGES

V   acuum sucked up granny's teeth.
O   h no, what are we going to do?
Y   ucky! Let's take a trip to the dentist.
A   re you going to help us?
G   et your vacuum and bring it here.
E   ven worse than I thought I'm going to
     need the drill.
S   uccessfully we got her teeth back.

Kelly Salvage (11)
North Frodingham Primary School

THE MAGICAL CARPET

My beautiful lilac purple magical carpet goes soaring through
the fabulous dark night.
It goes everywhere, it goes to all different countries.
I can see curtains shut for the night, children sleeping in their
lovely warm cosy beds.
I can smell the smells of fires burning and damp l eaves
I can hear dogs howling, cats scrapping and babies crying.
A young couple arguing and the leaves rusting on a glittery,
starry, shiny night.

Hannah Walker (8)
North Frodingham Primary School

VOYAGES

Voyages are fun,
On a boat or in the sun.
Voyages can be scary,
Angry bulls or fire-breathing dragons.
Going out in storms or defeating
cowboys in wagons
People think you're really crazy,
no you're not, we all have imaginations.
Sail the seas or go into space, but
remember, every voyage is fun.

Sarah Walker (10)
North Frodingham Primary School

My Voyage On A Phoenix

I flew on a Phoenix
Through medieval times
Saw battles over who to rule
I saw dragons flying through mid-air
Burning trees.

Saw messengers on horses,
Saw elves and dwarfs running through the woods
Went to a jousting competition,
Then I fell off the Phoenix and landed in bed.

William Doyle (9)
North Frodingham Primary School

A Wavy Journey

Every day I'm on the sea very boring all the time.
Over and under the waves I go
Think my dad has got seasick.
All the time the waves are swishing up the side of the ship.
The galleon is swaying in the wind
I don't know how Columbus could
Ever cope with this.
In the sea is definitely not the place for me.

John Wilkinson (10)
North Frodingham Primary School

BY ST THOMAS WATERS

I'd like to tell you of something that happened when I was a child
I was playing in the graveyard
So overgrown and wild

We wanted to go fishing but we hadn't a jam jar
I took one from the graveyard
We wouldn't take it far

We tipped out all the flowers onto the tombstone grey
We didn't really care
They were all dead anyway

We got quite bored of fishing we didn't catch a thing
I said let's run round the tombstone
To hear the dead men sing

We ran around the tombstone seven times then sang
Out into the graveyard
A blood cold voice out rang

What it said I could not say if I could I would not tell
I was absolutely terrified
I did not feel too well

We ran out of the graveyard and never went back there
Now that I am older
I came back here to stare

Please speak I ask the tombstone the voice just would not talk
And out of this old graveyard
I must begin to walk

I must begin to walk my memories are dead
Nothing else will happen
Or will it I said.

Lucy Davies (10)
North Frodingham Primary School

VOYAGE

V ery excited,
   Can't be late
   I'm going on a voyage
   I just can't wait.

O ver and over
   The waves we roll
   In our ship
   That's called the vole

Y nohting io fun
   But sailing is better,
   I nearly forgot
   To write my mum a letter.

A ll over the sea,
   We will go
   What will the weather be?
   Rain sun or snow.

G etting near to home
   I think I might cry
   I'll miss the red sunset
   In the lovely night sky.

E nding our voyage
   Will be very sad
   But to see my mum
   Then I'll be glad.

Lucy Pickard (10)
North Frodingham Primary School

PUB MENU

Steak:
Steak and mustard with garden peas.
Will make you get down on your knees.
Lovely onion rings in sauce.
Will make you run around a course.
Sweet:
With a lovely lovely crust.
It will make you say, 'I must'.
With this lovely lemon meringue
It will keep you away from the gang.
Drink:
With half a pint of rum.
It may tickle your tum.
With two pints of shandy.
It may make you dandy.

Christian Louis (10)
Laceby Stanford School

MY MICE AND MY DOG

My mice are cute and sweet
In the wild I wonder what they eat.
My dog loves his dinner
Everytime he's a winner.
At daytime during the week
My mice are always fast asleep.
My dog is always wandering around.
His bone still hasn't been found.

Lauren Grice (10)
Laceby Stanford Junior School

MY PETS

I've had many different pets in my life,
I've had rabbits, hamsters, dogs and mice.
But my favourite pet of all time
Was a little cat named Turpentine.

He died only a year ago
I still miss him, very much so.
He used to jump upon me in my bed.
The visions are still inside my head.

My friends were very nasty to him.
They used to throw him in a bin.
They tied him up and took him for walks
They even tried to make him talk.

I know one of 'them' killed him!
Because we found him dead, in a bin.
My cat didn't ever deserve it,
He wasn't even bad one bit.

Robyn Cordall (10)
Laceby Stanford School

S CLUB 7

S Club 7 are my favourite band,
And I think they're the best.
They perform on land,
And get more than one guest.

They travel from place to place,
Must be tired and sick.
Packing the same old cases,
The boss says do it all dead quick.

Their songs are loud,
They think they're not good.
But they get a big crowd,
Might be better if only they could.

Daniel Wilson (10)
Laceby Stanford School

MY FRIEND LISA

Me and my friend Lisa,
We both love to eat Pizza,
We go to town together,
We always play together.

We both love scary films,
They give us the chills.
We stay up late and wake up early,
To get some chocolate treats.

We both love sleepovers,
And playstations too.
We dance to Zombie Nation,
And sing to Leanne Rimes.

We share our secrets,
Problems too.
We will always be friends
Best friends too.

Jessica Sleeth (11)
Laceby Stanford School

SEASONS

Snow is settling all around,
Children playing in the playground.

Sun is shining through the trees,
Shining on the frozen leaves.

Spring is coming fast and steep,
And through the soil the flowers peep.

Summers come, and ice cream too,
Now no one here is feeling blue.

Autumn's here once again,
The day is drawing to an end.

Jessica Saville (11)
Laceby Stanford School

JACK FROST

In winter time you'll find that I go leaping everywhere
Sprinkling white powder all around
Over houses and on the ground.
I am capable of bursting pipes,
Flooding rivers and icy rain.
The children like me very much.
As they slip and slide around.

Sarah Pearson (11)
Laceby Stanford School

MY SATURDAY

Arrh! School! Boring!
No! It's Saturday.
Yes, bacon and eggs.
I can hear the bacon sizzling,
'Breakfast! Get up!'
So I get up, get dressed and go downstairs.
Course, it isn't ready, it never is.
I go upstairs again.
Turn on my playstation and set it up.
'Breakfast!' I turn off my playstation,
Go downstairs,
Eat my breakfast.
Then go to town.

Come home at 3 o'clock
Watch TV till around 6 o'clock.
Play a board game till around 8 o'clock
I don't like it but . . .
I have to go to bed at 9.30.

Ben Cook (10)
Laceby Stanford School

ALL ABOUT ME

There was once a little boy
Who always played on his Game Boy.
He played on pokémon card game -
And when he lost it was a shame.
He also played on pokémon pinball -
And his other hobby was playing football.

Martin Bowes (10)
Laceby Stanford School

FOOD

I like all types of food
burgers, beans and soups.
Sausages and chips
with lots of spaghetti hoops.

I like all types of fruit and veg
apples, oranges and lychees.
Potatoes, carrots and broccoli
But I can't stand peas.

I also like all types of sweets.
Sticky buns, biscuits and cream cakes.
Mars bars, twix and toffee crisp
And Cadbury's chocolate flakes.

If it's breakfast, lunch or evening meal.
A snack, a break or treat.
I'm really only happy
When I've got something nice to eat.

Ben Leeming (11)
Laceby Stanford School

FOOD

Brandy snaps and chocolate biscuits,
Strawberry ice cream with a flake,
Chocolate bars and fruit pastilles,
All of these I love to eat.

Putrid peas and gross green beans,
Sickening sprouts served with trout,
Broccoli is really disgusting,
All of these I hate to eat.

Chocolate ice cream is delicious
Served with apple pie it's nutritious,
Polos and wine gums are a treat,
All of these I love to eat.

Lauren Walker (10)
Laceby Stanford School

THE DOOR

When I open the door,
I see a crazy world of
plants and mammals.
It's a jungle out there.
With tropical birds, flowers
of all kinds dwell in its depths.
The anemone screams out with
its luscious colours.
A melody plays of strong vibrant
                        colours.
What a wonderful world.
When I open the door!

I look up to see nothing, just darkness.
This wonderful world has been darkened now.
All I see is one sad moment of my life.
I must have wasted this gift,
that God gave me now.
I see I am a wasted wreck.
This reality will shatter me soon.

No that cannot be right.
I must be lost in my thoughts forever!

Joshua Campbell (9)
Laceby Stanford School

My Poem In Winter

A cold but frosty morning it seems,
A cold but a nice day in a way,
The snowballs hitting on the ledge,
I love today I love this day.

Woolly hats and soft gloves,
Everybody looks the same,
The crunch leaves where the snow did not go,
It's almost like a game.

Thick coats and big boots,
The snow is just like cotton wool,
Everybody loves it. Everybody plays in it,
And after a good tea we'll all be full.

Next morning it's up to our knees,
All the parts of the snowman is done.
After all that fuss it's finally here.
But now look it's all gone!

Chelsea Wheeler (9)
Laceby Stanford School

Food

The Puddings
Ice cream with double cream.
Jelly bar with toffees and sweets.
Apple and bananas with jelly beans,
Lemon sherbets with apple foods.

Drinks
Apple soda, lemon soda all the drinks
you could think of in the world.
Coke Coke is the best you need Coke
All day long.

Christopher Pinney (10)
Laceby Stanford School

WARHAMMER

Warhammer is expensive,
But really fun to do.
When you're finished painting them,
You can battle with them too.

zBlood Angels and Black Templars,
Ultramarines, Eldar too,
Orks and Salamanders,
To give them a taste of doom.

Blood Bowl, Warmaster and Gothic,
All of the different games,
Epic and Nectaminda,
To play in different ways.

Warhammer is wicked,
I really like it lots,
All of the soldiers,
And all the cool robots.

Christian Cherry (11)
Laceby Stanford School

ME AND MY FRIEND

Me and my friend Jess love making a mess.
We do everything together and will do forever.
We go up town every Saturday
Especially on her birthday.
We eat chocolate and play games
And then we call each other names!
We have sleepovers and parties
And we eat all the smarties.
We watch scary films and play on the playstation.
We listen to music and make up dances.
We stay up till two am
And wake up at noon.
And play with balloons.

Lisa Clifton (11)
Laceby Stanford School

MY RABBIT MISTY

My rabbit Misty, she is white, black and brown
She plays with the things when I clean her out.
She plays in the run all day long.
She eats the wood on her cage all night long,
Misty is a greedy pig, she likes everyone,
She licks me and nibbles me, she loves me to bits.
Misty nibbles holes in my brand new jackets.
She is naughty but very sweet and she loves to eat.
Misty is clever and is very cute.
Bramble and Ebony are her friends.
Misty has long ears they are white and brown,
She is the best rabbit in the whole wide world.

Chloe Bett (9)
Laceby Stanford School

MY TOY ELEPHANT

My toy elephant is hairy and brown
My toy elephant has a really big frown
My toy elephant has a long nose
It always leads him wherever he goes
My toy elephant he's my best mate
You'll never believe what he just ate!
My rat, he ate that!

Thomas Davis (9)
Welton Primary School

WHEN THE SKY IS BLUE

When the sky is blue,
the birds sing in the sky.

When the sky is black
the birds go home to keep dry.

Jade Walker (7)
Welton Primary School

MY PUPPY

I love my puppy and she loves me.
We always play together.
And I take her for walks.
Once she did a tipple-tail,
So I did one too!

Nikki Dhatt (7)
Welton Primary School

A WINTER'S DAY

When I wake up on a winter's day,
I feel like I want to play,
but when I wake up what do I see,
a dark grey sky staring at me.
I quickly get washed then I get dressed,
hopefully I look my best.
With a buzz and a ring, what do I hear?
It's the postman delivering mum some more
                                junk gear.
A little bit later and I give a big sigh,
My brother begins to cry.
What's this, mum says
and then decides to take us on a car ride.

Elizabeth Singleton (8)
Welton Primary School

SPRING

The leaves grow on the trees,
Hear them rustle in the breeze,
Even when the spring sun shines,
It's cold enough to make you freeze.

Frolicking lambs in the farm at play,
Bounding playfully up and down.
The spring breeze is very nice
even though the roads are covered in ice!

Daniel Kemp (9)
Welton Primary School

THIS BOY AT MY SCHOOL

This boy at my school,
always flicks his food,
always calls miss a duedy-dued,
always tries to skip school,
he's a fool.
Always puts *kick me* stickers on people's backs,
always tries to get teachers the sack,
always tries to get other people into trouble,
but he gets double.
Never listens to our teacher
always make the chairs go 'eacheer'.

Vicki Turner (10)
Welton Primary School

UNTITLED

I broke me arm,
I broke me nose,
I broke me spine,
I broke me toes,
I thought I knew what I'd break next,
Not to my surprise it was my legs.

I hurt me shin,
I hurt me chin,
Well I'm *never* going skiing again!

Joseph Shawl (9)
Welton Primary School

WINTER'S DAY

On a winter's day
the sky became dull,
snowflakes falling
softly onto the ground,
white as chalk,
swiftly squishes under my feet,
the snowmen looked as if they were red,
        warm and cosy,
quiet as a mouse standing like a stuffed
            scarecrow!

Robert Barmore (8)
Welton Primary School

MY MUMMY

It was art day at school
I painted a red and blue splodge
And when it was home time
I saw a red and blue splodge.

She took me to her house
And she was my mummy.
She cooked my meal too!

At last I got into bed
The splodge was singing too.

Stephanie Thompson (7)
Welton Primary School

DREAMS

I have dreams
But they are not as they seem

I have dreams at night
Of my kite
Flying away in the distance

Some of my dreams are scary
And some have spiders that are hairy

Some of my dreams are funny
And some have lots of money

And that is all of my dreams.

Hannah Langley (9)
Wetwang CE Primary School

THE MAN FROM WETWANG

There once was a man from Wetwang
Who heard a massive great bang
And he bumped his head
On the back of his bed
And could not reach the phone when it rang.

Darren Ross (11)
Wetwang CE Primary School

Pets Nonsense Poem

Jasper the mouse he lives in a house
and he has a girlfriend called Shouse.

Roary the tiger lives in siliver and
he cleans up his miliver.

Wendy the elephant goes to pardovent
and she is so elegant.

Morise the rabbit lives in Hoarce's house,
he does and every time
he is scared he says 'Oh Borioo'!

Porky the pig wears a wig
he also wears a hig.

Clasper the cat chases the rats
and the bats.

Ben the bat he has a straw hat,
he does and he likes it so much.

Leanne Fisher (10)
Wetwang CE Primary School

Spiritual Kitty

He is the Spiritual Kitty
With his long ginger fur
And his claws on show
With a hiss and a purr.

When he slinks down the garden
He just looks so cool
A Spiritual Kitty
He is nobody's fool.

He's a streetwise feline
Who will always rule his patch
A Spiritual Kitty
He's never met his match.

He's our king of the alley
Topcat of them all
A Spiritual Kitty
His kingdon will never fall.

Natalie Wood (11)
Wetwang CE Primary School

NOTHING

Nothing is
as nothing does.
Nothing said
so nothing did.
Nothing was
as nothing says.
Nothing's not
til nothing's done.
Nothing takes
and nothing gives.
Nothing dies,
so nothing lives.
Nothing's gained,
nothing's lost.
Nothing never counts the cost.
Nothing ventured,
nothing won.
Nothing helps,
so nothing's gone.

Patrick Beauchamp (10)
Wetwang CE Primary School

My Dad

My dad's a sleepy head,
He just won't get out of bed.
It's half past ten,
And once again, he just won't get up out of bed.

My dad the sleepy head,
He just won't get out of bed.
I've tried smashing my toys,
And making a noise.
But he still won't get out of bed.
My dad the sleepy head
He just won't get up out of bed.
Driving! Driving!
Wow he's up! . . .
At 12 o'clock.

P Summer (10)
Wetwang CE Primary School

What A Busy Mum
Would Have In Her Pocket

1. A feather duster.
2. A tin of polish.
3. A sock.
4. A ten pence piece.
5. A Harry Potter Book No. 2.
6. A chocolate bar wrapper found on the stairs.
7. A mental maths homework sheet.
8. A photo of her little girl.
9. A pen and pencil covered in dust.
10. A calculator.

Zoe Hyde (10)
Wetwang CE Primary School

PETS

Porky Pig he wears a wig,
And he has a twig.

Casper the Cat is so friendly,
He has a wife called Wendy.

Harry the Hamster loves to eat,
His favourite food is meat.

Katie the Kitten,
Loves playing with her mitten.

Matthew the Mouse,
He lives in a house.

Scott the Seal,
He loves playing with his wheel.

Richard the Rabbit,
He loves to gabbit.

Tom the Tiger,
Has a friend that is a guilder.

Lorreta the lion,
Has a boyfriend called Ryan.

Kelly Fisher (10)
Wetwang CE Primary School

PETS

Pets can be strange and wonderful things
Have fur, or scales, or fins or wings
Fluffy hamsters that live in cages
Or hard-backed tortoises that live for ages.

Rats and mice that have long tails
Or even some people have house trained snails
Snakes that live in a vivarium
Pets need these habitats so be aware of them.

Corgi dogs for queens and kings
Or budgerigars with fluttery wings
Guinea pigs that squeak a lot
Pets are your best friends more often than not.

Cats with whos' tails twist and curl
Even hamsters pouches have secrets to unfurl
Parrots that repeat things that we say
And some pets surprise us in every way.

Charlie my hamster was ginger and white
He only used to wake on a night
But my new hamster Elderberry
Is she beautiful yes very.

So to conclude this poem well
There is one more thing that I will tell
Look after your animals, large or minute
Just remember all animals are cute!

Heather Lindley (10)
Wetwang CE Primary School

MY LIFE

I was born one year on November the 25th,
Eleven years from now.
I saw the world at 11.25am
Weighing just 7lb 14oz.

Eleven Christmas's I have had,
All exciting and fun, (ha, ha).
One of my best ones was Christmas 2000,
I got a keyboard, some clothes and a mobile phone.

I've had four holidays, all very good,
In 1997 I went to Euro Disney.
In 1999 I saw the real Santa,
In Lapland this was.

Two more holidays I have had,
Both to Spain in 1998 and 2000.
We flew from Manchester both the times,
Great both the holidays were.

I've rode horses, played hockey and learnt the violin,
All of these are good and fun.
The best of all is riding horses,
But with my friends is also fun.

When I grow up I want to run a horse farm,
With my friend Nat.
How fun it would be I hope,
My Life Has Been Wonderful.

Katie Rodger (11)
Wetwang CE Primary School